GA 10217
CW01652300
3-50
GL
10/26

Erin Kathleen O'Brien

AND A HISTORY OF IRELAND

Erin Kathleen O'Brien

AND A HISTORY OF IRELAND

Eileen O'Quin

Published in 1994 by
Riverstone Ltd.,
Ireland.

© Copyright Eileen O'Quin 1994

The right of Eileen O'Quin to be identified as the author of this work has been asserted by her in accordance with the Copyright, Designs and Patents Act 1988.

This book is copyright. No part of it may be reproduced in any form without permission in writing from the publishers except by a reviewer who wishes to quote brief passages in connection with a review written for inclusion in a newspaper, magazine, radio or television broadcast.

British Library Cataloguing in Publication Data

A catalogue record for this book is available
from the British Library

ISBN 0 9521265 1 6

Designed and Produced by Images Publishing (Malvern) Ltd.
Printed and Bound in Great Britain by Bookcraft (Bath) Ltd

To the obliteration of speech or quotation marks.
Silly little drunk tadpoles.

Chapter

ONE

A Celtic consciousness. A list. A sense of the ridiculous given sublime heights. A connection of nerve endings in brain cells. Small, synaptical explosions of revelation. Chemical messages of feeling and emotion. Cold connections of pure logic, drowned by gushes of endorphins. Euphoria, stimulated by experience. Learning from mistakes, snatching every opportunity. A perfectly designed form revealed amongst the confusion.

A respect for the power of words and a delight in trading them. Conversational gluttony. Impulsiveness, spontaneity, pessimistic fatalism. Charming and sociable suddenly turning moody and melancholy. A dread of money centred materialism consuming simplicity and nature. Sympathy for the misfortune of others, a long memory, and a belief that a wrong must be made right. Satirical, with a touch of malice. Mystical, and deliberately devious. A belief that the individual is ultimately important; that humanity means more than possessions; and that law was made for man, not man for the law. A well developed sense of honour and family. A fondness for witty talk, a good fight, and a good laugh.

A man with twinkling eyes, winked. He talked. He had not read her outstretched palm. He had not asked her name. No intrusion on her privacy, no interrogation of her background. A reminder that all men are equally created, and after that they are on their own. He disappeared like a legendary leprechaun.

Erin Kathleen O'Brien slumped at the table, a fist pressing distortion into her cheek. Her brain cells were undergoing execution by alcohol. Concentration waxed and waned, images distorted. The power of focus, sapped. A distant memory of her mother's death. An effort to stop time. Awareness was losing the battle as she slipped under the table. He searched the pub for familiar features. He rescued her from the floor, but was not able to arrange an easy partnership with the chair. The relaxed body is double the weight. She's not drunk, just looking for something, he announced to a disinterested audience. Chemical messages of coffee fumes.

I want to be drunk. I drank to forget. I don't want to be sober. I want to laugh and cry at the same time. I want to experience my grief, not deny it.

What can I do? he asked.

Make me laugh, pull faces, tell jokes.

I don't know many jokes, he said.

I do. Virginity, David, is like a balloon; one prick, and it's gone. She yelled. If God exists that's his problem! She screamed. Make your politicians work, don't re-elect them!

Desperation, despair, seized her. She allowed him to guide her to the door, past grins of a clientele knowing that alcohol talks loudly. She addressed a group by the door. This man is a medical student and he can't tell you why semen is white and urine is yellow. He winced.

Why's that, love? asked a woman with a man's hand on her knee. It's so that a man can tell whether he's coming or going, she winked. The man removed his hand. David propelled Erin outside to the strains of the group howling with laughter.

David, you're smiling. It's crude and coarse. And funny, she said, reaching for the support of a wall smothered in posters. An urban collage. Some words came into focus. The army builds men. I wish that they would build me one, she said. She stumbled, he supported her. She vomited, he waited. She sweated, he wiped her forehead. She gasped gulps of the cold, night air and tried to clear her lungs. Coughing, she announced to the empty street, I think that a fate worse than death is better than dying.

You are very witty, said David. And sad, said Erin.

Same pub, same table, next day. Erin sober. Regretting her drunken state only inasmuch as she did not talk more to the old man with twinkling eyes who had characterised her Celtic background. A connection made in memory cells; a feeling of having previously known; a curiosity as to what. A belief in a genetic memory that passes on information not connected to present environment. No conscious memories of Ireland. Early childhood sadness obliterated. A mother who wouldn't discuss it; a father forgotten. No particular feeling of deprivation, just a capricious desire to pursue the unknown. A decision to visit Ireland; time off from teaching; a vacation. David hesitant, cautious, anxious about the sea crossing. Momentarily amused by the memory of jokes screamed out on a previous evening. He had repeated them at a stag party that night.

David was right. The crossing from Liverpool to Dublin had the potential for re-arranging not only the stomach, but most of the body's freely suspended internal organs. Erin's suggestion of a journey to the cafeteria was so inappropriate as to be perverse. She explained that were they to throw up, it would be a suitable setting.

Stench of stale, fried food. A wall of rancid, musty, stagnant vapours to break through. Body odours and cloying, hot oil smells from the engine room, added to the fetid atmosphere of the ferry cafeteria. Erin valiantly struggled to keep her plate of french fries under control. David steered his solitary cup of tea, on a shaky tray, towards the only vacant seats. They sat opposite a washed out, worn out, woman, with two wailing children. The boat heaved, the tray slid. David struggled with the small piece of paper covering the hole on the triangular milk container. What a marvel of technology, he said, the paper has been welded over the hole! Erin's packet of ketchup had come from the same source. None of the ridges in the sealed top would tear to reveal the contents. David drank his tea black, and she ate plain french fries. The children opposite wailed continuously to a pale, oblivious, deaf, mother. Erin felt frustration building. She raised her fist and smashed it down on the milk container. Milk splattered across the tray, two drops landed in David's cup. She put the sealed packet of ketchup on the floor, and stamped on it. It oozed red. I've killed it! she screamed. The children stopped crying.

Erin and David headed for the deck. Cold, fresh air. Slippery floor, wet rails. David's complaints lost in a howling wind. Erin, distracted by the muscular, bent-over frame of a struggling deck-hand. A sinewy arm, gripping, tightening. The boat heaved, they lunged uncontrollably. David fell in a convulsed heap and refused help from the deck-hand. He and Erin had managed to roll with the motion. They glanced at each other with a quick recognition of mutual attraction, that had no past and no future. He was gone. Pride bruised, depressed, discouraged, rhythms upset, David looked to Erin for comfort and sympathy. She smiled. Murphy's Law says, that if anything can go wrong, it will.

Disembarkation at the docks. Blurred confusion. Feet on firm ground, body still moving. An enquiring voice. Where will it be now? A cheerful taxi driver. An old address on a faded letter handed to him. Going by the time of day, and everything else being normal, I will take you to the neighbour-hood pub. He looked at her in the rear view mirror. Desmond O'Brien, is it? I can see a resemblance. Anonymous streets, arrival, handshake, payment. Conn O'Connor's the name. I often stop by here myself when business is slow – that is my business – I hope to see you again, Miss O'Brien.

Frosted patterns on the glass windows that allowed penetration of day-light, but protected patrons from outside scrutiny. The pub is a sanctuary where conversation, companion-ship, and consumption, are linked in a trinity. A meeting place with behaviour codes and boundaries that should not be trespassed. Where a male can feel secure in the company of other men, and where he can speak without female interruption.

Erin went in first. Without any eye cast in her direction; without any head turned towards her; without any pause in conversation; she knew that she was an observed intruder. Logically, David questioned the barman about Desmond O'Brien, ignorant of the fact that local patrons can totally rely on the discretion of the barman as to their whereabouts. No luck, he said. It's not luck, it's skill, she answered. She realised instinctively, that although nobody appeared to be paying any attention, everyone knew who she was and what she was doing there. David returned to order drinks from a blank faced barman.

A man in elbow and knee posture at the bar, quietly enquired. Who would be wanting Desmond O'Brien? Do you know him? I might. What kind of answer is that? The only kind that you are getting. The man turned away.

Anyone would think that we were C.I.A., said David as he put down the drinks. You definitely look the part, smiled Erin.

Desmond O'Brien sat in the rented room of a tall terraced house whose past had been more promising than its future. Tired and disillusioned after a repetitive factory day, he mused on his attempt to persuade the foreman that a routine procedure was not needed. A brush off, with the usual dose of dislike. A resentment of Desmond's past, self employed and successful. Uppity, he had called him. That was his only reaction to the suggestion. The drive was no longer there to persist. He hadn't hammered at an ambition since his wife and daughter left him, but he stopped short of admitting it to himself. Make a living and forget to leave room for life. Daydreams through a window, disturbed. His friend Kelly was waving to attract his attention through the curtain gap. A win at the races? Whatever the urgency, Kelly wouldn't come inside. He might run into Mrs. O'Hagan, the landlady. That hag, O'Hagan, he called her. Desmond pretended not to notice. Desperate, Kelly came in on a softened foot. Is that you, Mr. Kelly?

Christ protect me, she can see through walls! Yes, it's me, Mrs. O'Hagan, how are you today? You'll be going to the pub, then? Kelly shifted his weight until Desmond appeared, deliberately delayed. Has he been behaving himself, Mrs. O'Hagan?

A voice came from behind the door, like the prophetess of doom. The way of a fool is right in his own eyes; Proverbs, chapter 12, verse 15. Let's get out of here, said Kelly, that woman has a way of ruining my whole day. That one was directed at both of us, said Desmond.

Out on the street Kelly was bubbling over with excited news. A girl was looking for Desmond, probably his daughter. No reaction. What's the matter with you?

I am immune. It's been seventeen years with no contact. As Mrs. O'Hagan would say. The heart knoweth his own bitterness, and a stranger doth not intermeddle with his joy. Proverbs, chapter

14, verse 10.

Inside the frosted glass barrier of the pub window, Desmond knew that the silent telegraph was at work. The intrigue was building. When he came in, his friends lingered and waited. Kevin O'Neill, with a glance and a nod of the head, pointed out where Erin was sitting. Desmond did not acknowledge. Kevin came over and offered to break the ice and make introductions. Michael O'Neill restrained his impatience with one look. Let the man make his own decisions. He'll be wanting to react gradually, commented Kelly.

If I trimmed myself according to everyone's wants I would soon be whittled away, said Desmond. A drink and some talk first. With a pint in his hand there was a gradual turn of the head in the direction of Erin's table. A swivel of his chair to take a longer look. A recognition of a familiar gesture. Yes, there was a look of the O'Brien about her

Who's the fella? asked Kelly. The boyfriend, said Kevin. I don't like him, said Desmond. All the jealous feelings of a protective father, towards a daughter, surfaced.

Kevin went over to Erin's table. Would you be the young lady who was making inquiries about Desmond O'Brien?

David, tired and irritated, accused Kevin of being rude and devious when he spoke to him earlier, at the bar. He's cheeky and flippant, thought Erin, and very good looking. She recognised a blaze of the eyes which precedes a flare-up, and decided to arbitrate. Thank you, sir, as soon as we have finished our drinks we would be pleased to join your table. Kevin raised an acknowledging finger and backed away.

Erin and David picked their way through an obstacle course of occupied tables and chairs. An introduction. An exchange of blank greetings, awkward emotions. The embarrassment of a public reunion. Then, as a sudden, nervous reaction, everyone was talking at once. Except Erin and Desmond, they exchanged two polite sentences and let everyone else speak for them. Kelly assumed master of ceremonies and with a leverage of questions pried open the previous seventeen years. Desmond leaned back in his chair and quietly and steadily indulged in his quota of prints.

Erin felt herself talk the same rocked back position and became temporarily detached as she watched and listened. God gave us two ears and one tongue so that we can listen more and talk less.

The only one in the group who was not playing This Is Your Life, was Michael O'Neill, he was obviously a listener. Erin noticed that he and his brother Kevin both had that attractive combination of black hair and deep blue eyes; but whereas Kevin was cheerful, sociable and charming; Michael was quiet, forceful and brooding. Definitely Heathcliff material; straight from Wuthering Heights. David wondered why Erin was pensive. He handed her a penny. I am thinking, David, that you have a lot of competition in this room, physically speaking. He smiled and nodded. Kevin introduced a new member to the group. A somewhat embarrassed Patrick Ryan, a visitor from America. Sandy blond hair with green eyes, rugged and personable. Square jaw, soap-opera material, thought Erin. But he is someone I could leave home for. He felt awkward, not part of the regular group, a loner by nature. An intellectual, said Kelly, with a touch of disdain. David and Patrick talked comfortably.

Someone commented that Kelly was on his sixth pint. It was, he explained, necessary, to take away the salty taste of the peanuts. He then complained that Desmond had not kissed his newly found daughter. That is because, said Erin, we are still getting to know each other. And anyway I don't like public displays of affection. Desmond nodded his approval. Not shy of speaking up. Like her mother, he thought.

Kelly discovered that they had nowhere to stay. There was a chaotic planning session. Loud disagreements. Alcohol narrowing the mind and lengthening the tongue. Eventually Kevin gained support for his aunt's boarding house so that Erin would be able to see her dad night and morning. Kelly begged off. He couldn't face Mrs. O'Hagan twice in one evening. She's a witch, he said to Michael. Don't make her out to be more exciting than she really is, he replied.

Her nephew, Kevin was one of the few people who could soften the resolve of Mrs. O'Hagan. He easily persuaded her to open up two more rooms for Erin and David. He mentioned the biblical quote about a good woman being above the price of rubies. His aunt was about to give him chapter and verse, but he had gone. The new tenants, overtired, staggered into their rooms. As she closed the door, Erin thought that the landlady was saying goodnight, but it was a biblical quote. Your old men shall dream dreams, your young men shall see visions. She didn't hear the reference.

Morning. Stimulation of consciousness, strong tea, car sounds outside. Erin peeked through the lace curtains. It's that taxi driver who met us at the docks. Conn O'Connor was more than a match for Mrs. O'Hagan. She pushed a damp strand of hair back behind her ear: wiped her wet, washing up hands on her apron; and silently let him in. Good morning, ma'am, would you kindly tell your two new lodgers that I am here to see them.

She went to the door of the front room – a small dining area, breakfasts only. He breezed in and offered the two surprised tourists a ride around the city. Conn insisted that Tuesdays were never that busy; explaining that it was a slow day; coming so soon after Monday, the least popular day of the week. They insisted on paying. He avoided the naming of an absolute sum. David said that they would fuel the taxi.

They couldn't have had a better guide. Conn was his own resource centre. Dublin was referred to in 140 A.D. as Eblana, by Ptolemy, but it didn't become a settlement until 871 A.D. It was the commercially driven Norse who decided that it was a strategic site and named it Dubh Linn – Dark Pool. Then the ferry that brought us over came from Liverpool to Darkpool, said David.

Erin sighed. She noticed plain, but attractive Georgian buildings. Conn continued. Dublin grew fourfold between 1700 and 1800 A.D. It was then that our major public buildings and Georgian terraces flourished. All in the name of commerce and the Anglo-Irish Ascendancy; and four Hanoverian kings of England called George. The slums grew at the same pace and were as barbarious and disgusting as the Georgian architecture was classical and elegant. These buildings look good, but at what a price!

They went to St. Patrick's Cathedral. Not Catholic, as Erin expected, but Anglican. David knew, he admired Jonathan Swift, satirist, who was Dean there from 1713 to 1745. He talked to Conn about Swift's comment when someone praised the virtues of Irish air. They said in unison. Hold your peace sir, lest the English tax it! They discussed the satirical and bitter pamphlet Swift published in 1729. A Modest Proposal For Preventing The Children Of Poor People From Being A Burden To Their Parents. He suggested that, as they were both poor and starving, the babies might be boiled and eaten. All said in the name of satire, I hope, said Erin. Yes, it was Swift's way of saying that the plight of the poor was desperate with no remedy offered by the rich. A nastier way of saying, Let Them Eat Cake, said David.

Swift was also the first Irishman to use the English language as a tool for the idea of a separate Irish identity, said Conn. He translated the Dean's epitaph, which was in Latin. Imitate, if you are able, one who did a man's part in defence of liberty.

Another church, St. Michan. A cranky, irritable, guide. Underground crypts. Bodies amazingly preserved over hundreds of years. Coffins and corpses. An atmosphere you could touch. A feeling difficult to verbalise. Outside, David wanted more than the experience, he wanted the reason. Conn said the church was built on the site of an old oak grove sacred to the Celts. He speculated that the slow decay of the oak released tannin into the crypts, which helped to preserve the bodies. Or it could be the magnesium limestone construction of the crypt which dries the air. Argument. Erin accused David of being unable to simply feel something without having a reasoned explanation. Conn stepped in to arbitrate.

Have you heard the story of the mother listening to the priest talking about marriage and motherhood? The mother turned to her friend and said, I wish to God I knew as little about it as he does. He broke the tension and they carried on with their tour.

They drove alongside the grey River Liffey and over O'Connell Bridge, broader than it was long. Erin noticed the names. Parnell, O'Connell, square, street, monument. She couldn't remember, but stayed silent. Nelson's monument was blown up, but a statue of Queen Victoria remains. It is ugly. That, said Conn, is called Ireland's revenge. David noticed the statue of Thomas Moore. You know – The Meeting of The Waters. See, it stands on top of the public lavatories near Trinity College, said Conn. Isn't that poetic justice!

The Long Room, Trinity College. The Book of Kells. Beautifully and painstakingly intricate. Eighth century. Erin kept quiet. David asked the inevitable questions, she wandered off. Conn suggested that it was lunch time. He would take them to one of Dublin's six hundred – or was it a thousand – pubs.

They passed the Bailey Restaurant, near Grafton Street. Conn pointed out that they had in their foyer the door to number 7, Eccles Street. Legendary home of Leopold Bloom, said David, where's the house? Gone to developer land, said Conn. Erin said that she couldn't get on with Ulysses and she didn't see anything of Dublin in it. David explained that it wasn't a travel guide but an emotional journey. Conn felt the beginnings of another flare up. He volunteered that Joyce himself had admitted that he wrote the book to keep the professors busy. And so it has. Joyce was the only expert on Joyce. His wife never read the book, she was not interested in his literary efforts. He gave her an autographed copy of the book and she offered to sell it to somebody. Joyce himself told Nora that there was not one serious single line in Ulysses. He delighted in controversy and being obscure. His contemporaries said that he was a nasty, anti-social, know-it-all. A bit like David, giggled Erin.

Inside the pub, a chance meeting turned into a social event. Chatter, gossip, endless, casual, frivolous. Erin gathered that a Dubliner is called a Jackeen. Rural people are called Culchies or Bumpkins. She and David mostly sat and listened. Business, politics, religion, all picked over with touches of sarcasm, wit, and a ready answer. A perverse structure in the gossip. Indirect, devious. The only topic to elicit a serious response was sport. The discussion of the performance of a horse, greyhound, football player, hurling or rugby team, had a sober tone. David was fascinated by the range and level of conversation. The tongues were well lubricated by whiskey and stout. Conn told him that the

Guinness in his hand was first brewed by the family of the same name in the eighteenth century. It was encouraged by the government of the time; they believed it would cut down on whiskey consumption. Of course it only complemented it. What do governments know. It rots the brain and shrivels the body, somebody said. What, alcohol? No, sex! Every time I see the statue of that priest who advocated temperance, it reminds me that I need a drink! Who would like stewed prunes? Get a bowl of plums and I'll breathe on them. Conn decided that a two hour lunch break was long enough and he guided his passengers to the door. Just when it was getting lively, said Erin.

Doorways. The doors in and around Fitzwilliam Square are so striking that someone made a poster showing thirty six of them. Another statue. What did he do? What does it say on the plaque? Nothing. Then that is what he did. The New Abbey Theatre built on the site of the old one. Talk of Yeats and the Irish Literary theatre. The cultural revival of the late nineteenth century. The guilt that Yeats felt when he thought that his words may have led to the Rising in 1916. The patriots didn't think so; they said they didn't read him. Another self-imposed exile. He went to live in England in 1922 when civil war came. They say he wrote some of his best poetry there. The literary Irish in exile, excel.

Storm clouds. The first few splashes of rain on the taxi window distorted the stark streetscape, which grew a dreary grey. In the distance, when visible, the hills darkened their green. At bus stops people posed with hidden heads. Sullen Lines. Some rebellious teenagers kicked an empty can, but the only anarchy was in the disorder of the disintegrated, dripping hair. Conn said that Irish rain kept the air fresh and the mind fertile, but played havoc with the traffic. Fortunately, he had a sixth sense about what other car's intentions were. He twice avoided an accident. It's not a driving test they need, but an intelligence test. He pointed out areas no longer safe, night or day. Dublin is not immune from the kind of urban violence in so-called civilised counties. We have our share of modern evils and the influx of tall concrete.

Mrs. O'Hagan, watching through the curtains; waiting, anticipating. The front door opened as the taxi splashed to a stop.

Tea, the elixir of the tired traveller. Conn had to leave. He lapsed into a brogue. Sure, 'tis choosy I am ma'am, but I do be enjoying your company. He winked a goodbye. Mrs. O'Hagan resumed her vigil at the veiled window. They have sown the wind, and they shall reap the whirlwind. Hosea, chapter 8, verse 7.

Desmond was not at home. If Erin wanted to see him she would have to go to the local pub, where he and his friends met most evenings, by silent, mutual agreement. David had the heavy, bleary, stuffy, feeling that is the precursor of a cold. He went to bed.

Patrick Ryan followed Erin into he pub. He was about to ask her about their tour of the city, when Kelly waved them over to the group. David was not well, she explained. She was not meant to hear the wry comment from Michael O'Neill about the effect of being in a taxi with a woman all day. Well, she remarked, a strange fate for men. They can't live with us, and they can't live without us. She had reacted with a raised, eyebrowed, shrug, that Desmond noticed. He remembered her mother.

Kelly wanted to hear about his hometown through a stranger's eyes. Conn was, said Erin, a charming guide. He has a useful balance of wit and information. Kelly interrupted, He's a scholar, you know. He's been through University – twice. As if once wasn't enough punishment! He speaks several languages, and is an authority on most subjects. He chooses to drive a taxi for the freedom it gives him . . . And don't forget my beautiful nature, said Conn, coming up behind him. A startled Kelly confused lecturer with lecherer and the group broke their concentration with taunts and comments.

Erin made a confession to Conn. Purged herself of the guilt of ignorance, admitted that the tour would have been more significant if the passenger had been better informed. Michael intervened, as if to split the intimacy. Then I suggest that this talented group do something about Miss O'Brien's lack of education. Let's make the teacher into a pupil. I will offer to teach her anything, at any time, in any place, said Kevin. He snuggled up to Erin and they laughed. Michael darkened, fearing ridicule.

Desmond intervened, sensing imminent blows. It's an

excellent idea. He raised a fist. The Strong Hand Uppermost, says the O'Brien motto. I will delegate subject and teacher. Patrick here is doing research at the university. He is American born. He can be objective about Irish history. He will not have the bias of one who was born and raised in Ireland. I choose him to teach Erin Irish history. I will ask Conn to teach her about our Celtic ancestors. Michael came up with the idea. I hear that he played around at school. I also hear that he could have been a top scholar if he had put his mind to it. Instead, he chose to apply his body to construction work. He knows a lot more than he says. He will teach her about Irish Catholicism.

Kevin whispered in Erin's ear. Michael's expression froze, revealing nothing. Erin decided that either he knew all about it, or he would scour the shelves of the library before his turn came. The group nodded a silent agreement to the chosen course of study. The Strong Hand Uppermost went into voluntary dormancy, and Desmond stepped down.

A gang of adolescent males nearby became rowdy. With a need to be noticed, they loudly exchanged prowess records across their table, with reference to various females. Erin knew, that as the lone woman in her group, it was partially for her benefit. The body language of the men signalled anger and impatience as the volume of the boasting increased. Some physical response was obvious, but this was their local, they didn't want to be the initiators of trouble. It was time to leave. Erin strolled over to the youths. Did I hear you fine lads talking about all those women you have slept with? Sleeping with someone is an innocent pastime; for it's not sleeping that you mean, but screwing, surely? And if it's screwing that you are boasting about, I'm sure those women yearned for it. 'Cos you look like a fucking group to me, that fails to satisfy; and if I were you I wouldn't be shouting about it. Erin's group bit their lips, and looked at the floor in unison as they filed out. Beyond the glazed windows, relief! Laughter spluttered forth. Patrick congratulated her for a unique way of stopping a conversation dead. Desmond's expression was a mixture of embarrassment and pride. Conn shook his head. Kelly was laughing so much he needed a pee.

Kevin tried to hide a partial blush. Michael, with a lopsided grin, managed a mock apology. I don't take back what I said about your companion being unwell because he had to spend the day in a taxi with you. Well, Mr. O'Neill, just hope and pray that what he has, isn't catching.

Chapter

TWO

Mrs. O'Hagan brushed past Erin with her wicker basket full of groceries. She didn't want to appear to be listening to the telephone conversation. She picked up the tin box next to the telephone. It rattled with coins donated for telephone calls made, not received. Erin ignored the gesture. Patrick Ryan was arranging an appointment for that evening, at his place, by firelight. That was the traditional setting for story telling, he explained. He would feel more comfortable if David was not present. Erin said that he had a convenient cold. She agreed to the assignation.

Mrs. O'Hagan was nursing David through his cold. She had glowed with achievement when she found out that he was a medical student. When she learned he was Jewish, she ceased her biblical quotations in his presence out of some misguided respect. Only Old Testament, Erin had warned.

While he had been housebound with his cold David had been victimised with a list of Mrs. O'Hagan's aches and pains, bunions, indigestion, arthritis, and rheumatism. He showed all the empathy of a trapped hostage. He sympathised and advised, listened and nodded, to her monologue. When he was well, he presented her with a potted plant. Mrs. O'Hagan thought that the sun shone out of his arse.

Erin needed to be alone. She went out for a long walk. Solitude, bliss; clarity of thought. Impersonal detachment, ideas flowing unimpeded. Time introduced reality. She stopped. Strange setting. Lost. Uncertainty. Car noises, curbside. Familiar. Can I offer you a journey, young lady? Conn, what a coincidence, I was lost in my thoughts. Strange setting . . . Hop in. Front seat, please. Back seats for passengers, front seat for friends. When are you in seeing Patrick Ryan? This evening. I'll take you there. He's a conscientious and likeable young man. Almost naive sometimes in his outlook. Talking of coincidences and Americans, I will tell you about an interesting chain of events. In the front seat of Conn's taxi Erin learned of the uncanny comparison of circumstances between the assassination of the American presidents. Kennedy and Lincoln. Lincoln was elected in 1860, Kennedy in 1960. Lincoln was shot on a Friday in the presence of his wife, and so was Kennedy. Lincoln's successor was named Johnson (Andrew) and was born in 1808. Kennedy's successor was also named Johnson (Lyndon) and was born in 1908. Lincoln's assassin, Booth, was born in 1839 and was killed (apparently) before a trial could take place. Kennedy's assassin, Oswald, was born in 1939 and was killed before he could be brought to trial. Lincoln's secretary, Kennedy, advised him against going to the theatre where he was shot. Kennedy's secretary, Lincoln, also advised him not to go to Dallas. Finally, Booth shot Lincoln in a theatre and ran to a warehouse; and Oswald shot Kennedy from a warehouse and ran to a theatre. Shivers ran through Erin. What is it they say? Someone just walked over my grave. That was really eerie, Conn. She reached for the radio knob. Let's have some music to brighten things up. She turned up the volume as Frank Sinatra sang, I did it my way. Oh, said Conn, they are playing the Irish national anthem. Gorbachev says its his theme song, but there's more than a little Celt in that one.

A passenger hired the taxi. As soon as he hit the seat he began a stream of chatter that was constant and unsolicited. Conn listened without comment in a manner that seemed customary. The passenger arrived at his destination and paid, while still talking. He thanked Con and waved goodbye. Sometimes, said Conn, I feel like a cross between a priest and a barman. I listen while people talk to unburden themselves. I have been told, in a ten minute taxi ride, someone's complete life story. I can only think that to pack it all in such a brief space of time, they must have rehearsed it before. They do not want a two way conversation, just a nod and a smile of recognition, to show that I am paying attention. They stopped outside Patrick's lodgings. Now, this one will only talk business. He is a naturally quiet lad and will not want you knowing details of his personal life. You'll have to come to me for that, he winked.

What about Michael, what's he like? asked Erin.

Introverted, introspective, and intricate. He doesn't burden himself at all. Sometimes you have to force the day of the week out of that one. Maybe he is compensating for the friendly, approachable manner of his brother, Kevin.

They had reached the row house where Patrick had lodgings. She was late. She thanked Conn for the ride, and climbed the front step, as Patrick opened the door. He had prepared a light supper, and encouraged Erin to eat, before the marathon began. Mostly, it will sound like a list, he explained. Simply because there is so much to cover. I am looking forward to it, my mind will be distracted from my research project. He didn't volunteer what that was. Watching television would do that, said Erin. Yes, but if offers no stimulation. She commented no further, hoping that she had stumbled on a compliment.

Patrick began. Erin paid attention. There is a prehistoric cemetery at Carrowmore, near Sligo, which has tombs that are 6500 years old. There may have bee eighty, originally, but a century of local quarrying for gravel, has reduced the number to thirty. Archaeologists are still working there, but the local council has chosen to use the quarry as a garbage dump. How progressive of them, said Erin. Another ancient site at Mount Sandel, south of Coleraine, in County Derry, is 6600 years old, but we don't know where these people cam from, or what happened to them. The first farmers arrived here about 5600 years ago. They cleared land, farmed it, made pottery and wove baskets. They were also technically skilled and used stone tools, chisels and adzes. They buried their dead in stone burial chambers, covered with earth, called court graves, found mostly in the north.

Forty eight hundred years ago more immigrants arrived. They buried their dead, communally in passage graves, similar to those found in Brittany and Portugal. We do not know very much about lifestyle then but gold jewellery found indicates advanced technique. Basically our information about ancient Ireland is very sketchy, although we do have the legacy of grave sites.

Newgrange, just north of Dublin, is the largest and most impressive megalithic tomb in Europe. It is an earth mound, thirty six feet high, shaped like an inverted saucer, enclosing a large chamber, entered through a narrow passage. The entrance passage is lined with slabs of stone and is sixty feet long. It opens into a circular chamber, twenty feet high. The roof box above the entrance is a design marvel. It allows the winter light of the sun to shine into the central chamber only at the winter solstice; the day before, and the day after. Yet the passage is curved. At those times the sun's rays illuminate three linked spirals, incised on the wall.

It reminds me of a similar phenomenon in the Chaco Canyon, New Mexico. The Anasazi Indians also tracked the winter solstice. At that time, a beam of sunlight shone through two enormous slabs of stone and struck two spiral patterns on the cliff face. Then there are the ancient earthworks at Poverty Point, Louisiana. Six great octagons, arranged one inside the other. Passages radiate out from eight corners. If you observe down these passages at the correct times, a special position is pin-pointed of the sun, moon, or a star. These ancient, astronomical, calendars, including the Pyramids, Stonehenge, and Newgrange, were all constructed about the same time, 2800 B.C. Unless there was some global communication network, one can only speculate that guidance was given for such technically sophisticated devices. I have wandered away from my topic.

Erin nodded. No matter, it is fascinating. We must discuss at some other time the fact that the Theory of Evolution is just a theory, and does not allow explanation of humanoid footprints that have been found side by side with dinosaur prints, and in other extremely old rock formations. Patrick smiled. Back to Ireland.

Over a cup of cocoa he said that in old stories Newgrange was called the Brugh (house). The mound was once covered with thousands of white quartz pebbles that have disappeared over the years. Quartz plays a part in short wave radio transmission. It controls the frequency of radio waves. I am about to wander again, so let me return to ancient Ireland by talking about legends. Stories that were passed down for centuries, and eventually written down by monks in the seventh and twelfth centuries. They were Christians, and wanted to make the old stories tie in with biblical history. So they added their own stitches to the embroidery. The first recorded people, they said, were a sect descended from Cham, son of Noah. The people were known as Cessair, and according to Giraldus Cambrensis, a Welsh cleric, they were descended from Cesara, Noah's granddaughter. When she heard about the flood, she sailed for the farthest islands in the west. Only her ship survived, carrying three men and fifty women.

At least they got the proportions right, commented Erin.

The group next mentioned are the Partholonians, who, presumably, had survived the flood. Ireland was divided by Parthalon's sons into four. The first adultery was recorded. Partholon went away on a hunting trip and left his wife with Toba, a friend. She seduced him, and when Partholon found out, he killed her dog. This was the first recorded act of jealousy and revenge. In her own defence, the wife said that the adultery occurred because he went away and left her. The first judgement then made is reminiscent of the Indian law of Manu, which says that the adulterous wife throws her guilt on her negligent husband. Are you following? Patrick smiled down from his chair, to an intent, fire-glazed, knee-hugging, listener on the floor.

I've drunk my cocoa, and yours is cold, she responded. What's next?

The Fomorians, said to be a race of demons. There is no arrival record. They had a battle with the Partholonians, but did not wipe them out. A plague did that; killing nine thousand of them, and leaving the Fomorians to tackle the next invaders, the Nemedians. They came from Scythia. They cleared the land and created twelve plains. When the inevitable battle came with the Fomorians, they lost. As a penalty, they had to pay, every November an annual tribute of two thirds of their cattle – and children! Finally they conquered the Fomorians in a battle, and killed the leader, Conann. But the Nemedians were so depleted in number that they left the country.

The Firbolgs came next, a Belgae tribe. They divided the

country into five, and introduced metal weapons, a judicial system, and kings. They had no trouble with the Fomorians, but were defeated by new invaders, the Tuatha De Danann. They conquered the Firbolgs, but allowed them to stay in the province of Connacht. They compromised at first with the Fomorians but finally defeated them at the second battle of Moytura. The Tuatha De Dannan – people of the goddess Danu, or Diana – were said to have come in boats, and in clouds through the air. These people give the original stories of fairies or little people. They brought the coronation stone, Lia Fail, to Tara. They, in turn, were conquered by invaders called the Sons of Mil, or Milesians. They were defeated at the Battle of Tailtu, and were said to have then gone to the land of the Young, Tir Na N-Og, westwards across the sea from Ireland. The ones who stayed, retreated into mounds and became the hill folk, or sidh, of Irish legend.

The Milesians arrived from Spain. They reached Kenmare Bay in thirty ships. There were nine brothers. Five were killed by storms, and four landed. One was Amergin, who sang the song of Creation . . . beautiful poetry. The Milesians were the last pre-Christian conquerors, the Celts. They have a fascinating history and mythology, but I understand that this is Conn's subject.

Let's have a rest, said an enchanted Erin, stretching. Patrick yawned, and stared into the fire.

These legends seem to correspond roughly with groups of pre-historic people, said Patrick, starting up again. The Fomorians could be original Stone-age inhabitants. Partholonians and Nemedians could be Neolithic farmers. Firbolg and Tuatha De Danann, could be Bronze-age. The Milesians, Iron-age Celts.

Now a little about Ireland, as a known place. It was called Ierna in a Greek poem from the fifth century B.C. Classical authors called it Hibernia and Juverna. Some think that it could have been the land of the Hyperborians referred to by the Romans. Plutarch called it Ogygia, meaning, most ancient. In Sanskrit, it was referred to as I Hiranyi, translated as Island of Sun Worshippers. Some say that the word Eire is derived from the Indo-European word Piera – meaning fertility. In poetry, the word Banba refers to Ireland in the heroic sense. The word Fola is used for the intellectual sense.

Ireland has also been called Inisfail: meaning Island of Destiny. Scotia is another name, from Scotia, a Milesian woman. The Tuatha De Danann had a queen Eire, and the Milesians called the land Eirinn. A son of Mil, called Ir, ruled in the north-east. From him, and his two brothers, Heremon and Heber, are said to be descended all the noble families of Ireland. Scandinavian invaders in the ninth century, called the land, Irland, or Irlanda.

This is all terribly romantic. Patrick, I even heard my name mentioned, said Erin. Although my eyelids are drooping, if you are willing, I would like to hear some more. Patrick had to lubricate his throat with something a little more potent than cold cocoa.

Leaving legend and picking up so called history, at least recorded history; we know that the Celts, arrived around 350 BC. They were Goidelic Celts, and they gradually imposed their language and law upon the whole island. A Celtic leader, called Conn of the hundred battles, formed a kingdom called Meath, in the middle of the country in 200 A.D. Tara, was its capital.

Was that who our Conn was named after? asked Erin.

I don't know, said Patrick. I think that this mother gave him the name because it means intelligent, and she considered that important . . . The Irish word for province, means fifth. The others were called Ulster, Leinster, Munster, and Connacht.

From the middle of the third century, A.D., the Irish raided and settled the west coast of Britain. Turmoil in Europe, during the fourth century A.D., saw refugee scholars from Bordeaux and Nantes, settle in Ireland; in Leinster and Munster. Plague brought refugees from Britain in 664 A.D. There was still a maritime link with Spain, going back to the Bronze-age.

Erin could feel a glazed expression creeping over her face. It's 1:00 a.m. and we have only just started. Patrick gasped. I can't move, she said, I'm full of knowledge and sleep. Can I stay, Patrick?

A flash of embarrassment crossed his face. Yes, I'll sleep on the couch.

No, I will, said Erin, I'm the intruder, you take the bed. I have to be at the university at 9:00 a.m., but there is no need for you to get up then. We will meet again tomorrow night.

Yes, said Erin, and she waved four floppy fingers in a good night gesture.

A knock. A jump. Strange surroundings. Temporary confusion. She had stayed the night. Who was this? It's me, said Conn. I've come to collect you. An open door. A heavy headed, bleary eyed, Erin. This reminds me of a tombstone that Kelly once saw, he said. The engraving said, I still live. Kelly commented that if he were dead he would at least own up to it! You sit down young lady and I will fetch some tea. The liquid tannin stimulated recovery. Conn said that he was her chauffeur today. Erin went back to her room for a wash and change – skilfully avoiding Mrs. O'Hagan – and she and Conn set out for Newgrange.

Patrick smiled at his student. How was Newgrange?

Eerie, I felt as if I had seen it before, or something like it. You didn't mention the large boulder near the entrance; textured with dots, carved with spirals, concentric arcs, and diamond shapes. The spirals remind me of galaxies, she said.

Erin, I have so much to cover, I can only give superficial treatment. But I am pleased that you took time to see for yourself. My teaching has aroused your interest, that is all I can hope for. It was five o'clock. He would talk until ten, and pack as much as he could into five hours. He lay the paper and kindling for the fire.

The seventh and eighth centuries were a time of learning and craftsmanship in Ireland. A Golden Age when movements such as the Celi De were founded to create poetry and elaborate stone carving. This surge of vitality could have achieved a pre Renaissance revival if invaders had not caused chaos and confusion. The Irish could not relax in cultural sophistication, they had to defend their lives and property. Many scholars fled to Europe. They took books and manuscripts with them. That is why there are more Gaelic manuscripts in European collections than there are in Ireland. The Irish were not prepared for the united aggression of the Vikings. The country was divided into one hundred fifty small kingdoms or tuaths, that frequently fought with each other. The attacks began around 795 A.D. in coastal areas, and by 830 A.D. they had pushed inland.

The Irish called the Vikings from Norway, The Fair Strangers.

The Danes were called The Dark Strangers. Invasion eventually led to settlement. In 841 A.D. Dubhlinn became one of the first, followed by Cork, Limerick, Wexford, Waterford and Wicklow. The invaders integrated with the local population, took Irish wives, and introduced surnames like Bolan, Sigerson, Elliffe, and Tormey. They also brought Scandinavian trade and commerce techniques.

There was a Viking governor of Ulster called Turgesius, around 830. He added Meath and Connacht, and eventually became Abbot of Armagh. Those Vikings who stayed integrated with the Irish, who were a fractionalized bunch anyway. What they did not try to do was govern and control them from Scandinavia. In fact, when Danish ships attacked Dublin, the Irish king of Ulster, helped the Vikings there to fight back. By the middle of the tenth century, they controlled mid and southern Ireland. Don't think that the locals were happy about this. They planned to fight back.

You, being an O'Brien, must have heard of Brian Boru. Erin nodded. The O'Briens are his descendants. He came from a tuath in north Munster called Dal Cais, you may hear him called a Dalcassian king. He was the younger brother of the ruler, Mathgamain, they went south to recapture lands taken by the Vikings. They retrieved Cashel in 964, and then Limerick. Ivar, the deposed king in Limerick, paid an assassin to murder Mathgamain. Brian became king. He went after Ivar and defeated him and two Eoganacht princes; Donovan and Maelmud.

Meanwhile, in the north, King Malachy fought the Vikings and captured Dublin. He mistakenly put the exiled Olaf's son. Sitric, in command. Brian realised that to consolidate his strength he would have to challenge Malachy.

Malachy would not fight, he conceded, and Brian Boru proclaimed himself Ard Ri. This was the closest Ireland ever came to being united under one man. However, he was an elderly man and he had not groomed a successor. Maelmorda, a king from Leinster, decided to ally with Dublin's Sitric, and king Sigurd of the Orkneys. They would challenge Brian.

The mixture of families was confusing. Maelmorda's sister, Gormlaith, had been married to Brian. He divorced her in 995. In all she was married three times, including to Olaf. Sitric was their son. She plotted with her brother and son to overthrow Brian. They planned to fight on Good Friday 1014, as they thought that he would be reluctant to fight on a holy day. They met at Clontarf, and Brian's side was victorious. His sister, married to Sitric, observed the battle and made sarcastic comments about the drowning Vikings that were driven into the sea. Sitric slapped her so hard that he knocked out her tooth.

The victory was not sweet for Brian Boru. As he was seventy-three he had been advised to stay in his tent. A retreating Viking, Brodar, found him there and killed him. Norse sagas say then when Brodar was caught, his stomach was split open, his entrails nailed to a tree, and he was made to walk around it. However, the Irish did not use this torture, but the Vikings did. Brian Boru was buried beside the High Cross of Armagh.

He had introduced hereditary surnames to Ireland. The prefix Mac – meaning son of – and O' – meaning descendent of. Boru was the small settlement that he came from, but the sept took its surname form Brian. Their place of inauguration was Tullagh, in County Clare. The Earl of Inchiquin, Marquis of Thomond, and Baron of Burren has his seat at Dromoland Castle, in County Clare. He has a continuous line of descent from Brian Boru.

As well as consolidating power, Boru also introduced the Bardic Order. A new lay order, that would teach. This Order would influence Ireland for five more centuries. Up until that time, learning had been dominated by the monasteries. The Vikings who remained became assimilated into the population.

Break time. An absorbed Erin confessed that she had heard little of this before. In English classrooms, anything to do with Ireland is always referred to as the Irish Question; accompanied by a degree of irritation and contempt. There was no background and no follow up. Ireland was only mentioned when there was a rebellion, and it was looked upon as a rude interruption to English affairs.

Patrick sighed. Yes, history is probably the most biased subject taught. Each country has its own version, and it is taught so that it is unrecognisable to another country that was involved. I try to be objective, but I am obviously telling Irish history with a subjective interest. And with that I push on.

After Brian's death. Malachy ruled as Ard Ri until he died in 1022. No one strong leader emerged and the power struggle began again in the provinces. The O'Briens were based in Munster, at Kincora Castle. They had periodic challenges from the MacCarthys who were descended form the old Eoganacht kings of Cashel. The O'Connors ruled Connacht from their capital at Rathcrogan. Except for a small area in the northeast, called Brefne. This was ruled by the O'Rourkes. Ulster was divided into three. The tuath Tir Eogan was ruled from Tullahoge, by the MacLochlainns. The tuath of Tir Conaill, was ruled by the O'Donnells. To the east and south, there was a dispute over the ancient kingdoms of Oriel and Ulidia; between the O'Carrols and the kings of Tir Eogain. The ancient kingdom of Meath was fought over after Malachy died. The province of Leinster was ruled over by the MacMurrough family after 1042, when Dermot MacMurrough became king. Is that clear Erin? She smiled. I smell a power struggle, what happened to the Arid Ri?

Brian's great-grandson, Murtagh O'Brien, ruled from 1086-1119. He was quite competent. Turlough O'Connor succeeded to the title in 1136. He and his son, Rory, gave Ireland the closest thing to feudal administration that she had ever know. Rory, in fact, was the last Ard Ri and he died in 1198. But I am jumping ahead of myself. I have to go back to Dermot MacMurrough, who was the king in Leinster. He had two wives, but when he was forty-two, he abducted the forty-four year old wife of Tiernan O'Rourke. Some say Derbhorgaill gave her consent, and it was no abduction. Anyway, a year later she returned to Tiernan, I'm not sure under what circumstances, and he wanted revenge.

Is this brewing up for a storm? asked Erin.

Indeed it is, the stage has been set for an invasion from England. Tiernan finally conquered Dermot, who decided to ask Henry II for help. He found him in Acquitaine. He had Norman ancestry, and tended to spend a lot of time in France. The Normans were originally Vikings who had settled in France, and been granted their own territory, Normandy. A Norman duke, William, had been victorious in England in 1066. His grandson, Henry, II, had a problem with his own Norman barons in Wales. They were land hungry, and quarrelsome. For the illegitimate ones there was no land to inherit. The name – Fitz – was given to illegitimate offspring of royalty. This request of help from Dermot MacMurrough was a useful tool.

Then there was the question of Rome and the Pope. There had been many disagreements with Ireland over the matter of church doctrine. Rome was also claiming rent called Peter's Pence. Supposedly, one penny for every house, to be paid to the Holy See, under the jurisdiction of the Donation of Constantine. This said that all islands converted to Christianity had to come up with this rent.

Politics and economics rear their heads again, said Erin.

Politics, indeed, said Patrick. The Pope in question being Adrian IV, who was an English Cistercian monk, Nicholas Breakspear. The first, and only English Pope. Henry obtained a Papal Bull from him giving the Vatican's blessing to the invasion. It has been said that this Bull was a forgery, because Henry II had been out of favour with the papacy since the murder of Thomas à Beckett, and no concessions would be given to him. Another discrepancy is that the Bull was not used until 1171, and Pope Adrian died in 1159.

That would not be the only time that a crucial document was a forgery an Irish history, commented Patrick.

Dermot landed in Leinster with a small force of Normans in 1167. Rory O'Connor was not aware of the intrigue, and actually restored part of Dermot's kingdom to him. He asked for two sons as hostages, which was customary. Dermot gave up two sons, knowing that he had invasion plans. When the Normans arrived, those sons would be executed. One heir remained, Donal Kavanagh.

In May, 1169, Rober Fitzstephen and Maurice de Prendergast landed in County Wexford, with six hundred well trained men. Dermot waited for reinforcements. One year later, Maurice Fitzgerald, Raymond Le Gross, and Richard de Clare (Earl of Pembroke) otherwise called Strongbow, landed near Waterford with one thousand more men. With their military strategy, they took Waterford, and Strongbow married Dermot's daughter, Eva, in the cathedral there. They captured Leinster and Dublin for Dermot, but he did not live to use these gains. He died the following spring, 1171. Strongbow named himself King of Leinster.

Henry II decided to go to Ireland in 1171 to make the English presence official. He took the Papal Bull. Strongbow submitted to Henry at Waterford, was given Leinster, but only allowed to administer Dublin, Wexford and Waterford. Hugh de Lacy, a friend of Henry, was given Meath and made Viceroy. He divided the kingdom among his officers; de Cussac, de Nogent, de Cyrs, and Planchette. The de Burgos family went to Connacht. Do you recognised any Irish surnames?

Yes, but they changed.

Right, Cussac became Cusack, Nogent-Nugent, Cruys-Cruise, Planchette-Plunket. The de Burgos became Burke. Other surnames with Norman origins are: Fleming, Roche, Fitzgerald, Carew, Barry, Joyce, and Dalton. In the eyes of the Irish people, this Norman Invasion was the beginning of the English involvement in Irish affairs. The memory is long. In 1969, a monument was erected at Baginburn to commemorate the Norman landing of 1169. It was smashed a week later.

A strange event was the submission of the Irish Kings to Henry. McCarthy of Desmond: Donal Mor O'Brien, of Thomond; O'Rourke, of Brefne: O'Carrol, of Oriel: O'Dunleavy, of Ulidia; all submitted. Only Rory O'Connor, the Arid Ri, refused to do so. I can only speculate that they agreed if they did this he would go home quickly; and he did. He left in April, 1172. Those kings did not realise the serious implication of their submission. They had a Celtic background and no tradition of written agreements. The documents held little meaning or consequence. Or, so they thought.

Without Henry II and his Norman barons, Ireland might have evolved into an independent Celtic kingdom. As it was, the English king had been accepted as ruler of Ireland, with no bloodshed.

It reminds me of the way that the North American Indians were tricked out of their land as well, said Erin. By written agreements that were meaningless to them. She yawned. No reflection on the lecture, sir, nor on the seriousness of the topic, but it is ten o'clock, and I have to go. We have covered five hundred years, not bad. But tomorrow the years won't go by so quickly. More happens.

I have set aside every evening this week. I am finding it quite a challenge. I am sorry that I have put your social life on hold, she lied. She had heard that two dates had been broken on her behalf. Poor Patrick had been accused of lying by one irate female, when he explained that he was teaching history to a woman friend. And I suppose that you think that I call my pet Zebra, Spot, she had said to him. Conn was Erin's source of information. In the same breath he told her that Patrick was much in demand among the more attractive females. She also learned that he was divorced. She had not dared to mention it.

Putting my social life on hold is no inconvenience, he volunteered. What I need most, Erin, is somebody to make me do what I can. He squeezed her hand. She left.

It was becoming quite the little ritual. Erin arrived at Patrick's place, they would chat informally for a few minutes while he put the kettle on, and lit the fire. Then they would talk history.

Before long, fighting broke out between the Normans and the Irish. Peace was negotiated by Laurence O'Toole, Archbishop of Dublin, between Rory O'Connor and Henry II. As a result, the Treaty of Windsor divided Ireland into two portions, with Rory ruling Connacht. Then, surprise, Rory agreed to submit to Henry as ruler of Ireland, and pay an annual tribute! The first English betrayal: Henry did not keep the terms of the treaty. He gave away the very land he had promised to Rory. Rory had to fight for his rights.

In 1175, Henry's seventeen year old son, John, came to Ireland. He went on a binge of handing out land to his friends. Where Norman barons died with no heirs, he took over. A sizeable part of Munster which by right belonged to the O'Briens, was given to John's Butler, Theobald Walter. He took the title Earl of Ormond, and the family name, Butler. A large area, south of Tipperary, was given to William de Burgo, founder of the Burke family. He married an Irish girl, Donal Mor O'Brien's daughter. The western part of Limerick, plus a large part of Kerry, went to the Fitzgeralds. They founded the title, Earl of Desmond. In the north, the old kingdom of Ulidia, went to the de Courcy family. The kingdom of Oriel, formerly O'Carrol property, went to Bertram de Berdon. Tir Conaill and Tir Eogain were the only small kingdoms left in Irish hands. In 1230, Gilbert de Angulo, got control of Tir Eogain. His family later changed their name to Costello. The Viceroy organised a parliamentary system whose members were mostly Norman, and the first parliament met in 1254.

Socially, the Normans were fitting into Irish life, away from English control. They adopted Irish ways, including tribal bickering. Gradually they came to resent English interference. They did not like England using Ireland as a source of revenue and manpower for fighting wars in Scotland. The Irish realised that if they were to ever get their land back, they would have to improve military techniques. They imported mercenaries from Scotland, called gallowglasses, who were well organised, with battle technique and equipment. The man behind the effort was Donal O'Donnell, the only Irish leader in control of a small kingdom, Tir Conaill. Before he died in 1281, he had regained Brefne.

The next event is some Scottish treachery from Robert the Bruce. He had defeated the English at Bannockburn in 1314, and knew that the money for the English campaign had been siphoned from Ireland. He suggested to the Irish Kings that an invasion by the Scots could work in their favour. Maybe they thought that it would help drive out the Normans. His brother, Edward, landed at Larne in 1315, and with Irish help, defeated Richard, the Red Earl of Ulster. By some strange means, Edward had himself crowned king of Ireland in 1317. Then Robert arrived with more men, and the Irish realised that all was not well. They were convinced when the Scottish army plundered in Ulster.

Just a minute, interrupted Erin. How did they allow a foreigner to crown himself like that?

The Celts did not have hereditary kingship. They were used to accepting a show of strength from an outsider to claim a throne. But, on the other hand, they also knew when a take-over was underway.

It was the new Viceroy who drove the Bruce army back. Probably under urgent orders from England, to take advantage of the Scotch-Irish split. Robert returned to Scotland, but Edward continued to fight, and was beaten at Faughart in 1318, by John de Bermingham. His head was sent to Edward II in England. Viceroy Mortimer complained to Edward II about the lack of support when called for; and was replaced by Lionel, Duke of Clarence, Edward's son.

Meanwhile, the Normans were building castles; Maynooth, Carrickfergus, Dublin and Trim. Clergy were increasing in number and sat in parliament. Normans adopted language, culture, and customs of the Irish. The Viceroy, Clarence, reported this swing away from English influence in 1361. The English were worried by what they could see as an erosion of their power and influence, so they introduced the Statues of Kilkenny at the parliament there in 1366. The statues forbade alliance with the Irish by marriage, concubinage, and fosterage. Anglo-Normans were not allowed to be entertained, speak, ride or dress in Irish fashion. They were ordered to practise religion separately. Irish clerics were not allowed to be presented to a cathedral or collegiate church. The national sport of hurling was banned.

Don't you think that they could have made these statues a little more restrictive? said Erin.

Do not jest, he replied, these were the first of a series of acts imposed by the English that were designed to deter and humiliate. Did society grind to a halt? No, in true Irish style the statues were mostly ignored, and things went on as usual. Clarence left, and the new Viceroy, Gerald Earl of Desmond was an eminent Gaelic scholar and poet.

Richard II went to Ireland in 1394 to investigate the gradual claiming back of land by the Irish. The Irish kings made all sorts of promises to him that they did not intend to keep. They had learned how to play this game from the English. Content that he had solved the problem, Richard returned to England. During fighting in 1398, the Viceroy was killed and Richard made the mistake of returning to Ireland. While he was away, Henry of Lancaster claimed the throne.

Have you heard the expression Beyond the Pale? Erin nodded. The Pale was the area just around Dublin where Anglo-Irish influence remained strong. Anything beyond this area was in Irish and Gaelicized Norman territory, and considered to be barbaric by the English. In northwest Ireland, the O'Neill, O'Connor, and O'Donnell families were back in control. The O'Doherty, O'Reilly, O'Kelly, O'Rourke, MacDonnell, Magennis, MacSweeny families, had all regained some control of their land. The dominant Anglo-Irish families were the Butlers of Ormond and the Fitzgeralds of Kildare and Desmond.

In 1449, Richard, Duke of York, took the position of Viceroy, and his son, Edward, was born here. Although he did not stay long; he returned in 1450, he had seen the country that he would deal with as monarch. At a Drogheda parliament he had granted parliamentary independence and asked for loyalty for himself and his son. In 1459 he was defeated, and in 1461, his son became Edward IV.

Edward had James, Earl of Ormond, beheaded, because the Butler family had supported the Lancastrians. The Butlers and the Fitzgeralds sat on a power see-saw. Thomas, seventh Earl of Desmond, was made Viceroy. The Anglo-Irish families complained that he was a Gaelic supporter, and had him replaced by John Tiptoft. He had the Earls of Desmond and Kildare, arrested. Desmond was beheaded, and Kildare escaped to England. He told the king of the treachery, was pardoned, and reinstated as Earl. After Tiptoft, Thomas Fitzgerald was Viceroy, and when he died, his son Garret More took on the position. It was 1477. Have you heard of him? Erin shook her head. His speciality was uniting Anglo-Irish and Gaelic families by marriage. His sister and five daughters married into the O'Neill, O'Carrol, MacCarthy, Butler and Burke families. He was so well connected, he could have claimed the title king. But he didn't

Does 1485 ring a bell for you, Erin?

Yes, Battle of Bosworth, Richard III defeated by Henry VII.

Let me tell you what this meant for Ireland. This Henry, grandson of Owen Tudor, Welsh blood, forgot the promises once made to his native Wales. Having risen to power at the English

Court and married Elizabeth of York to unite Lancastrians and Yorkists; he was determined that Ireland would not be a place of conspiracy against the Tudors. In 1494 he replaced Garret More as Viceroy with Sir Edward Poynings. His instruction was to restore Ireland – to whole and perfect obedience.

Sounds ominous, said Erin.

It was. He began his plan for subservience by the introduction in 1494 of Poynings Law. He removed from the Irish parliament, independent legislation. The English parliament had to ratify any law they passed. The Statues of Kilkenny were re-introduced. But, he was re-called in 1494, owing to a well connected marriage. Garret More Fitzgerald, who had been held in the Tower of London, was re-instated as Viceroy. While in London, he had taken as his second wife, Elizabeth St. John, who was the cousin of Henry VII. He had first to sign a declaration to observe the laws introduced by Poynings. No doubt he had his fingers crossed behind his back, while he did so. An O'More, from Leix, killed Garret More in 1513. His son, Garret Og, known as Young Gerald, succeeded him.

Henry VII was just as determined as his father to keep Ireland subservient. He replaced Garret Og in 1534, because his son, Thomas was tricked into believing that his father had been killed, and he rebelled. Silken Thomas, the tenth Earl of Kildare, and five of his uncles, were executed in London in 1537. The Kildare family and Fitzgerald power was dwindling, and the Butler family saw their opportunity to rise. Henry said there would be no more Irish Viceroys.

Sorry to keep on about these Viceroy people, Erin, but they directly represented the English king, who shaped Irish history at this time. Do you have any questions?

Yes. Was there any chance, in spite of the Edward and Robert Bruce fiasco, of Ireland and Scotland uniting against England?

If there was, it disappeared when the king of Scotland was killed at Flodden in 1513. Previous to that, Celtic links had been destroyed when James of Scotland, hanged the Lord of the Isles, John MacDonnell, and his three sons. After two hundred fifty years, the title was no more. There could be mutual sympathy, but not much chance of alliance. O.K. tell me about the swinish things that Henry VIII did.

He included Irish monasteries in his dissolution policy. Strangely, he did not ban Catholicism. I have always thought, that in spite of his formal break with the church of Rome, Henry was a covert Catholic. Politically, he forced the Irish aristocracy to swear allegiance to him and give up their lands, which he then returned as feudal grants. He hoped to create chaos and division. He made Gaelic royalty take English titles. Murrough O'Brien, became Earl of Thomond; Donough O'Brien, became Baron of Ibrackin; Conn O'Neill became Earl of Tyrone. He abolished the Brehon law system, which struck cruelly at Irish tradition. As an example; the law of land tenure-tanistry – where a successful family member claimed the land – was replaced by the law of primo-geniture, where the eldest male inherited property, whether he deserved to or not. In 1541, a special parliament was called to legalise these acts. The proclamations had to be read in Irish and English, because only the leader, the Earl of Ormond, understood the English version As a finale, Henry had himself officially named King of Ireland. The crowning insult for the Irish people. This would probably be a suitable time to take a break, suggested Patrick. We can tackle Elizabeth I before Conn collects you at ten.

After cocoa, Patrick talked of restrictive education practices that forced Irish priests to seek education in Europe. Colleges were founded to educate them at Salamanca, in 1592; Lisbon, in 1593; Paris, in 1605; and Rome, in 1625. No wonder Irish priests make such good missionaries, they have a history of being made to leave.

A quick word about the mother of Elizabeth I, Ann Boleyn. She was the granddaughter of the seventh Earl of Ormonde. She was brought up at Carrick-on-Suir by her cousins the Butlers. Through them, she was connected by blood with the O'Briens and O'Reillys. These O'Briens became Protestants. Elizabeth had more than a few drops of Celtic blood, but very little Celtic sympathy.

The Tudors were determined to break Ireland. In another attempt to undermine Irish culture, Elizabeth I asked Gerald, fourteenth Earl of Desmond, to suppress the fili. She said that wandering poet-storytellers were seditious. They represented a powerful class in Gaelic culture. These bards orally preserved Irish customs, laws, and stories, by roaming the land, talking and singing to the people. By 1603, there were few fili left.

Shane O'Neill had reclaimed the O'Neill title in 1562. He fought with the MacDonnells in Antrim, and the O'Donnells in northwest Ulster. He was beaten, and fled to Scotland, where he was murdered by relatives of the MacDonnells. He had a famous nephew, Hugh O'Neill. For six years, Hugh had lived in England as a ward of the Earl of Leicester. He had been to court, and was known and liked by Elizabeth. But Hugh was nobody's fool. He knew that the English were conditioning him. He remained true to himself and Ireland. When he returned, he witnessed the failure of one rebellion in 1580, led by a Desmond, using Spanish and Italian troops. Hugh decided to ally with Hugh Roe O'Donnell to fight the English. O'Neill had married Mabel Bagnal, sister of the Viceroy, Sir Henry. The Viceroy had been firmly against the marriage and he hated Hugh O'Neill.

The two Hughs beat the English army in 1598 at Yellowford. The English called it the Battle of the Blackwater, and were outraged at the defeat. Elizabeth, in her fury, ordered the Earl of Essex to Ireland to gain a victory. He arrived with twenty thousand troops in April, 1599. By July, his force was reduced to four thousand men after several small battles. One thing that he is remembered for is a massacre by his troops on Rathlin Island. Children and elderly from the MacDonnell family had been sent there for safety, the English soldiers did not spare them. When a depleted Essex reached Ulster he made unofficial peace with Hugh O'Neill. Elizabeth, enraged, recalled Essex and had him beheaded.

Then events turned against Hugh, Irish chieftains switched loyalties after deceitful tactics. The O'Connor betrayed the Earl of Desmond, after a forged letter led him to believe that it was to be the other way round. Another deceitful plan sent Art O'Neill and Niall Garr O'Donnell over to the English side. Some say that Niall deserted to the English because he was jealous of cousin Hugh's appointment as Earl of Tyrconnell. Either way, Niall did not benefit by his defection. He was imprisoned in the Tower of London from

1609 until his death in 1626. The Englishman, Carew, from Munster, contacted the leader of the Spanish troops in Kinsale. He persuaded Don Juan D'Aquilla, to be uncooperative. The Spaniard had been sent to help the Irish, but threatened to leave if they did not join him in Kinsale. They were at the other end of the country, but three exhausted divisions, under O'Neill, Tyrell, and O'Donnell, went to Kinsale. Charles Blount, Lord Mountjoy, beat the weary Irish in 1601, at Kinsale. The Spanish did not fight. Many Irish troops died in battle, and all prisoners were executed. Hugh O'Neill asked for mercy, and an ailing Elizabeth granted it. His luck ran out. She died, and James I was said to be planning a conspiracy charge against them. Mountjoy had the O'Neill inauguration stone destroyed at the family seat in Dungannon.

Hugh O'Donnell fled to Spain, and died in 1602. Rory O'Donnell, his brother, and Hugh O'Neill made a monumental decision. With the prospects of being merely tenants under English dominance, or of being imprisoned and probably killed, they decided to leave Ireland permanently. Ninety-eight Gaelic aristocrats left altogether, with their families, to settle in Europe. They went on September 14, 1607. It was called the Flight of the Earls, and was a major turning point in Irish history.

Gaelic royalty had left a Gaelic peasantry to their fate. They had to cope without their traditional leaders. Socially, they had to adapt without cultural role models, or patrons of the arts. Those who had stayed had to find their own solutions. Meanwhile, Europe had an infusion of Irish blood and talent which I will tell you about tomorrow. It is five to ten, and I hear Conn's taxi outside.

Miss O'Brien you look drained, what is it?

I'm just getting over the Flight of the Earls, Conn. I suppose I can see why they did it, but where was that Irish – let's stay and fight it out spirit?

I guess poor old Hugh was justifiably fed up, said Conn. There he had fought the English for nine years, and only lost one battle at Kinsale, through no fault of his own; and they called that defeat. Then Murphy's Law got him, and everything that could go wrong, did go wrong. He was chased into a corner, and chose to leave.

I am reminded, said Erin, of the saying – Put not your trust in princes – Machiavelli, wasn't it?

Ah Machiavelli. He was the advocate of settlements, too, as a political weapon. Has Patrick got into that yet?

No, he just finished Elizabeth I.

Oh, her, have I got a piece of information on that one! But you know, he winked, they say that Machiavelli was really an Irishman anyway. He was called MacKelly, and he changed it to a more Italian sounding name . . . Now, about Elizabeth . . . have you heard of the Bisley Boy? Erin shook her head.

The story goes that Henry VIII didn't like to see Elizabeth at court. She reminded him of Ann Boleyn. He sent her to stay with a noble family at Overcourt, near Bisley, in the Cotswolds. They say she caught a cold there during the winter, and died. They knew that Henry would blame them so they looked for a girl to substitute for the dead child. The local people helped the family look, they didn't want the burden of Henry's rage. The only child who was suitable, was a seven year old, red-haired boy, who had also studied Latin, like Elizabeth. That is why, in spite of the determination of the Tudors to ensure the survival of their dynasty, Elizabeth remained a so-called Virgin Queen. She went bald in middle age. Have you ever seen her in profile? Very masculine. Sure, she had her favourites, but we won't discuss what she did with them. This century, a stone coffin was dug up at Overcourt; it contained the skeleton of a young girl. The skeleton disappeared, but the coffin is probably still there. The locals still call Elizabeth I the Bisley Boy . . .

In those times it was customary to perform an autopsy on a dead monarch. Elizabeth left strict instructions that no such autopsy was to be performed on her body. As far as I know, those instructions were obeyed. Erin's mouth had fallen open; she pushed her jaw closed with a fist. No wonder she told everybody that in her breast beat the heart of a king!

She didn't tell Patrick about the Bisley Boy the following evening. She would save that. Instead she opened with a question. Why didn't Elizabeth try to force her Protestantism on Ireland?

Patrick explained that it was a political decision. The new religion was promoted, but conservatively. To force it would have drive the Anglo-Irish and the native Irish, closer together. It was also the reason why Elizabeth did not actively pursue a plantation policy. Both sides objected, and agreed they were against it. But there were some plantations founded in Leinster, Munster, and Ulster; introducing such names as Carew, Deveraux, Beamish, and Daunt. However, by founding Trinity College, Dublin, for Protestants only, Elizabeth made her point.

James I, although descended from royal Scottish blood, continued to undermine the Irish. He never knew his mother, said Erin, so he had no family tradition. He owed allegiance to England and it was said he was indifferent when Mary Queen of Scots was executed. His was another questionable birth. He may have been fathered by an Italian courtier, Rizzio. Whom he resembles.

He actively planted Ireland, said Patrick. In an act of pure treachery, he seized all the lands of the Earls who left for Europe. He said they were traitors and had taken part in the 1601 uprising. He ignored the fact that they had been officially pardoned in 1603. Thousands of acres were taken, in six northern counties.

The rules were: English plantation settlers were allowed to lease land to English and Scottish Protestants. The Scots settlers were allowed to lease to Protestant Irish, but at double the rent to the Crown. Native Irish lessees had to pay triple rent. Derry was given to a group of London companies who called it Londonderry. By the way, in 1984, it was officially called Derry again.

Settlers were concentrated in Ulster, because O'Neill and O'Donnell lands were confiscated there. Ulster also contained areas of particular significance to Irish Catholics, such as Armagh. These plantation settlers created a new landlord class, but they were never partially accepted by the natives, as the Anglo-Irish Catholics in the south had been. In fact, Catholicism was the only thing that the Irish had left. The English had encouraged them to give their religion a prominence in their everyday life, that it would not have otherwise assumed. Their leaders had gone to Europe, they looked to their church for guidance. The priests became the new community leaders, and had the respect and loyalty formerly given to the kings and earls.

Question, said Erin. You did not mention Edward VI, and Mary, when you did the Tudors. Edward was only around for a short time, but in his reign the Pale was enlarged to include Offaly and Leix, in 1547. Mary was Catholic, but did not do much for Ireland. She did rename Offaly, Queen's County, and Leix, King's County, after removing the O'Connors and O'Moores from this midland area. She then gave their estates to English settlers. She said that after her death they would find Calais written on her heart. Let's change that to Ireland, said Erin.

Back to the sixteen hundreds. In 1603, Belfast was founded on a Chichester grant. He was a Viceroy with a particularly corrupt government. The plantation continued, by 1622 there were seventy-five hundred British settlers in the Counties of Antrim and Down. In the six Ulster Counties there were thirty-seven hundred settlers, half English and half Scottish. Sir Walter Raleigh owned a huge plantation area, including confiscated Desmond estates, in Waterford, Cork, and Tipperary. He introduced the potato to those estates. We all know what disastrous effects that would have. He did sell that land, as I believe he found the locals somewhat uncooperative.

The plantation settlers, sent by James, had pushed the native Irish towards the Shannon. In North America, incidentally, colonists sent by the same James, pushed native Indians towards the Alleghenies . . . The Irish were now subject to English law, including judges, sheriffs, and tax-collectors. These officials replaced clan rule, and what had been a tribal society.

Question, said Erin. What happened to the Irish who went to Europe?

The played a significant part in European history, but I can best explain that later. For now, the English court received a report in 1614 that there were three thousands Irish soldiers fighting for Spain in the Netherlands, and they were excellent fighters.

Chronologically, we have reached the times of Charles I. The Irish thought that he might be sympathetic, because he had a Catholic wife. What they didn't know was that he wrote to Henrietta Maria in 1645 that – Ireland must at all times be sacrificed to serve the Crown of England . . . and then set out to practise what he had preached. In 1627, he instructed Lord Falkland to offer Catholic peers and bishops in Ireland, the purchase of Graces. They were only to be offered to the Old English, people of English descent. These Graces included the permission to practise law. He collected £120,000 for his depleted treasury. Then a lobbyist group successfully petitioned against the issuing of the Graces. Charles withdrew them, but did not return any of the money. The disgusted Old English group joined with Irish Catholics and called themselves Confederate Catholics.

Thomas Wentworth, an efficient administrator, was sent to Ireland in 1632. His task was to generate prosperity that would yield some revenue for the English treasury. He threw out corrupt people in Dublin, and extracted £70,000 from London merchants who had been withholding payments. He introduced polices of trade development and industrialisation. By 1636, he had a treasury surplus of £50,000. He had a trained peace-keeping force as well. He had been too efficient and successful, and had made enemies in England. Politics is treacherous, and competent people have to watch out for their backs; or in those times, their heads. His enemies saw to it that he was charged with treason. It was not proved, but he was beheaded anyway.

The anti-colonist feelings were growing in the north. By 1641, the Irish were ready to rebel. One rebel was Owen Roe O'Neill, Hugh's nephew. He had gone to Europe in 1607, and had fought with the Spanish in the Netherlands. He had also seen battle at Yellowford at seventeen; and at Kinsale, when twenty. He returned to help the uprising in Ulster, and was given command there. The man who was given Leinster, a General Preston, was known to Owen from his time in the Netherlands. He did not like him. Lord Castlehaven, an English Catholic, commanded in Connacht. Too many different factions, each with their own interest. The plan was to seize Dublin on October 23, but an informer leaked this to the government. Dublin was not taken. In 1646 Owen Roe had a brief victory at the Blackwater River, that his uncle, Hugh, would have been proud of. Colonists held out in a few places, including Londonderry and Carrickfergus.

This was the same time as the English Civil War, said Erin.

Yes, but it was nearing an end, said Patrick, and the Irish were learning to take advantage of an English disadvantage.

Oliver Cromwell came to Ireland in 1649 to teach the Irish a lesson for earlier rebellions, and because he knew there were many Irish troops willing to go and fight for the Stuarts. Of interest, is the surname, Cromwell. It had been assumed by Oliver's great-grandfather, nephew of Thomas Cromwell, Earl of Essex. Although Oliver was born in Huntington, England, his family had Welsh origins and the family name had been Jenkins.

In Ireland, his campaign was utterly ruthless. He landed in August, with twenty thousand men, many veterans of Civil War battles. Three weeks later, when Drogheda refused to surrender, he took it by storm, and killed three thousand people, one thousand alone in the local church. He marched to Wexford, gave it an hour to yield, stormed it and killed three thousand more. He said that by terrifying the land into submission he would save further bloodshed; but actually he was deliberately brutal because he did not like Catholics and because he did not have time to spare.

He was needed for more killing in Scotland. His solution to stop further rebellion was to annex Ireland, abolish its Parliament, and confiscate three quarters of its land. Officers in his army were rewarded with some of this land. Catholics were ordered to go to Connacht or face execution. To Hell or Connacht the expression was. Irish forces did not surrender until 1652, the destruction death, and bitterness, endured. Irish people, including children, were sent as slaves to Barbados, Montserrat, and Virginia. It was estimated that six thousand Irish boys and girls were dispatched as slave labour. Another thirty thousand people left for voluntary exile in Europe. Many were soldiers. Cromwell's name is hated and cursed to this day. Fucking Ironside, they call him. Of the land that was taken, some went in payment to English troops, much of it went to English absentee landlords, who had financed the campaign. In 1641, Catholics held about sixty percent of the land. By 1665, they held twenty percent, and most of that was in Connacht. The new, landed, ruling class of Protestants after 1653 evolved into the Protestant Ascendancy. The working class Irish were virtually in bondage.

What happened when the Restoration brought Charles II to the throne? asked Erin.

He was honour bound, said Patrick, to assist the people who had remained loyal to his father. Many Irish had fought on the Royalist side, yet Charles II had no real liking for the Irish. Those who had obtained land under Cromwell, now paid homage to the new king, and made sure they got seats in the Irish Parliament. It was the Viceroy, The Earl of Ormond, who instigated the Second Act of Settlement, whereby a claims court assessed the status of seized land. Catholics who had their land restored had to prove that they have never been involved in any rebellion against Charles or his father, yet the Puritan followers of Cromwell were to receive compensation for land they had to give up. The Act of Explanation of 1665, removed, and redistributed about thirty percent of the land seized under Cromwell. Two thirds of the fertile land remained in Protestant hands. The Church of Ireland, modelled on the Church of England, catered to less than ten percent of the population, yet it was the only one permitted to hold public worship. It levied tithes for its support on the whole population. Because the English farmer did not like competition, in 1665, the export of cattle and horses from Ireland, was stopped. Followed by meat, butter, and meal. Some good things did happen; a plan was laid down for the city of Dublin, and Phoenix Park was begun. It was much expanded in 1747, by the Viceroy, Chesterfield. The park is seven miles in circumference, and has seventeen hundred acres.

It's beautiful, said Erin. I have walked there. Where did the name come from?

It's a corruption of the old Irish word, *fionnuske*, meaning, spring of running water. Historically speaking, we have a lull. Not too much to report until Charles died.

In 1685, he was succeeded by his brother, as James II. He was supposed to abide by the Protestant way, but he actively patronised Catholicism. His two daughters, Mary and Anne, were brought up as Protestants, but when a son was born, he had a Catholic training. The English were becoming restless, and looked for a suitable substitute. In 1688, William of Orange, ruler of

Holland and married to James' daughter, Mary, landed in England. The government had offered them the throne. James had little support, and left for France on Christmas Day, 1688.

Meanwhile, in Ireland, Richard Talbot, Earl of Tyrconnell, appointed by James as Viceroy, was raising an army. James arrived from France, in March, 1689, with only a few French soldiers. They lay seige to Londonderry by blocking off the River Foyle to English ships.

I have heard of this, said Erin. The thirteen apprentice boys who held out for one hundred five days; it's portrayed in English history as an heroic event. James shouldn't have bothered, she said, he should have used storming tactics like Cromwell.

Anyway, Patrick continued, two British ships relieved them and James moved south to the Boyne. He met his son-in-law, William, there in the summer of 1690. Actually, said Patrick, it was a poor excuse of a battle, not well organised, but William did win. With the help of his English, Dutch, Danish, German, and Huguenot, soldiers. Although James went into exile, to France, after that battle, the war was not over. Patrick Sarsfield was left in control, and defended Limerick. He only surrendered to prevent further slaughter. Eighty-five percent of the garrison there had already been killed. There was an encounter at Aughrim, where a Dutch general, called Ginkel, defeated a French general, called St. Ruth; and that was an English victory! Not very decisive, really. After Limerick, Sarsfield, negotiated, in good faith, the Treaty of Limerick. The terms under which he surrendered, included an agreement for Catholic toleration in Ireland. There was never any intention, by the English, to keep the terms of this Treaty. Sarsfield, disgusted by this deceit, left for France, with fourteen thousand Irish troops. This exile was called the Flight of the Wild Geese. There is a refrain in a poem by Rudyard Kipling which I am reminded of . . . Patrick quoted.

Old Days! The wild geese are flying;
Head to the storm as they faced it before!
For where there are Irish there's memory undying,
And when we forget, it is Ireland no more.

You might be interested to know, he continued, that the Pope of the time, Alexander VIII, was involved in a political argument with the French king, Louis, about the freedom of the Gallican church. Louis supported James II, and the Pope made it clear that he supported William of Orange, a Protestant. When William was victorious, the Pope had a Te Deum sung.

With friends like that, who needs enemies, commented Erin.

The Wild Geese left behind many women and children. Irish held land fell from twenty five percent to fifteen percent. In France, Irish troops charged into battle against the English yelling Remember Limerick! In Ireland, insult was added to injury by the introduction of the Penal Laws, designed to squeez every last drop of human dignity from the Irish. Patrick reached absent mindedly for Erin's hand. I feel myself becoming less objective than I had planned, he sighed.

I forgive your lack of objectivity, said Erin. I could not be objective either, if my memory contained a chronology of rebellion, treachery, punishment and exodus. I would like to hear about these laws, I do not remember their content.

Edmund Burke said it best . . . The Penal Laws were a machine of as wise and elaborate contrivance for the impoverishment and degradation of the people, and the debasement in them of human nature itself, as ever proceeded from the perverted ingenuity of man . . . Burke's mother was a Catholic; his father, a Protestant lawyer, had probably converted to escape these laws. From 1695, for thirty years, these laws were in force. Of course, Catholics could convert. The laws said that Catholics were to be excluded from all forms of public life. Parliament, the legal profession, the civil service, and army, universities and schools. The Catholic Clergy was banned, and the few priests allowed, had to be registered. Catholics were forbidden to acquire land from Protestants, either by purchase or inheritance. For the few remaining Catholic landowners, they were ordered to divide their land equally among all children, unless the eldest became a Protestant. Then he could inherit it all. If a Protestant, landowning woman married a Catholic, she forfeited her land to her Protestant next-of-kin. A Catholic was not allowed to send his children abroad to be educated. He was not allowed to own a horse valued at more than ten pounds.

I am appalled, said Erin, at the ignorance, and prejudice of the minds that devised those laws. Nothing like this has ever been enacted in England. No wonder the Irish are reputed to have a healthy disregard for the law. Anybody who had to exist in those conditions would react that way. How else can you deal with such degradation?

Well, it strengthened Irish Catholicism. It was practised in secret, tenaciously. At the time of George I, a bill was introduced by the Irish Privy Council, to castrate any unregistered priest found entering the country. Only diplomatic pressure from France prevented the passing of this bill. Unregistered priests were in great danger, but were also seen as heroes. They celebrated Mass behind a curtain, so that their congregation could not identify them to authorities. Mass was also celebrated in the open air of the countryside, to avoid detection. Education took part there too, in Hedge Schools. Teachers were in danger if discovered; they accepted any kind of donation as payment. The Irishman called his grave a Protestant Lease. Time for a break, Erin. Let's have something to lift our spirits.

This reminds me, said Patrick, raising his glass, of those Irishmen who went abroad. He consulted his notes, briefly. Richard Hennessy went to France from County Cork in 1740, he founded the famous distillery in Cognac.

The soldiers who left continued to fight, some to command. Ulysses Brown commanded an Austrian army. Marshall Leopold O'Donnell was Captain General of Cuba and Minister of War for Spain, in the 1840s. John Barry commanded the first naval battle of the American Revolution. William Brown founded the Argentinian navy. Don Ambrosio O'Higgins became Governor of Chile, and Viceroy of Peru. His illegitimate son, Bernardo, threw the Spanish out of Chile and became the first President. Peter de Lacy was a Field Marshall in the Russian army. His son, Maurice, held the same position in the Austrian army. Cornelius O'Rourke became a Major General in the Russian army. His son, Count Joseph, was one of the Russian generals who fought against Napoleon. Field Marshall Conn O'Donnell was Governor of Transylvania. Andrew O'Reilly was Governor of Vienna, and Alexander O'Reilly was Governor of Louisiana. The O'Neills went to various places, including Portugal. One descendant, Jorge O'Neill, a Portuguese nobleman, lives in Lisbon. Henry Clarke was a Minister of War for Napoleon, his cousin, Oliver, Baron of Pierreborg, was a general in Napoleon's army. Edme Patrice MacMahon was Marshall of France, and President from 1873-1879. Thomas O'Gorman from County Clare was a friend of Louis XV, but lost his estates during the French Revolution. He returned to Ireland and became an enthusiastic antiquarian.

Next, I will explain how Irish emigrants affected early American history. Along with the Penal Laws went trade restrictions. English wool manufacturers lobbied successfully for restrictions in 1699. This trade embargo affected Protestants as much as anybody. Scottish Presbyterian settlers resented Anglican authority. Between 1718-85 more than two hundred thousand Ulster Presbyterian settlers emigrated to North America. These Scots-Irish were aggressive colonists. They tended to treat the native Indians the same way that they had treated the native Irish. They never hesitated to open up new frontiers, and produced such pioneers as Davy Crockett, Sam Houston, and Stonewall Jackson. Presidents with Scots-Irish backgrounds include: Andrew Jackson, Polk, Buchanan, Andrew Johnson, Grant, Arthur, Cleveland, Harrison, McKinley, and Wilson. It took the Catholics a little longer to get established politically. However, native Irish and Scots-Irish, both recognised English restrictions when they saw them. They all played ardent parts in the War of Revolution. Four signers of the Declaration of Independence were born in Ireland, five others were of Irish descent. The Declaration was first printed by John Dunlop, who learned his trade in Strabane, Ireland. Twenty-two men of Irish descent sat in the first Continental Congress. In England, Lord Mountjoy said, after the Revolution, We have lost America to the Irish. Thomas Jefferson had a toast – Here's to Ireland, may she soon sever her fetters, and take her place among the free Republics of the Earth.

As a direct result of the American War of Independence, some concessions were given to Ireland. The restrictive trade laws forbidding the export of woollen goods, were repealed in 1780. In 1782, the subordination of the Irish Parliament to the English Privy Council, was ended. The administration of Ireland was to be by an English appointed Lord Lieutenant. A group called the Irish Volunteers were formed to defend Ireland's coast, they were mostly Protestants. In the country, Catholic peasants formed terrorist groups to protect their interests, called Whiteboys and Defenders. The repression continued. Absentee landlords sent agents to demand rents from tenants. In the north, the so-called Ulster custom, gave tenants there the right of tenure and sale. In the rest of Ireland, a tenant who improved his holding, had his rent increased.

Around this same time, 1780, secret bands of Presbyterians formed in County Armagh. They began by intimidating landlords, gradually they became an anti-Catholic group. In 1795, they renamed their group the Orange Order, after the William who had won at the Boyne. When there was talk of Catholic emancipation, in the nineteenth century, they held annual marches of solidarity in July, to commemorate the Boyne. In 1885, the Unionist Party was born at a meeting in an Orange Hall, in a response to demands for Home Rule. Here, I have a copy of the Orange Oath, said Patrick, reading – To the glorious, pious, and immortal memory of good King William, who saved us from rogues and roguery, slaves and slavery, knaves and knavery, from brass money and wooden shoes; and whoever denies this toast may be slammed, crammed and jammed into the muzzle of the great gun of Athlone, and the gun fired into the Pope's belly, and the Pope into the devil's belly, and the devil into hell, and the door locked and the key forever in an Orangeman's pocket . . .

I see you smiling, Erin, but to the Orangeman this was a serious oath. Patrick closed the book. That's enough for tonight. He leaned back in his chair and closed his eyes. He rubbed them, he sighed. Did I go on too long?

I wasn't looking at the clock, said Erin. I am sorry that you are exhausted, it is tiring talking so long. I feel guilty.

Don't, he said, it's not this evening. I get lost in the telling, I enjoy it. I have other pressures. Things that I can't burden you with. Erin would have asked, but she felt that she did not know this introverted, sensitive, American well enough to intrude. They sat in a dimly lit silence, until Conn's taxi pulled up outside. She squeezed his hand goodbye, as she left.

I don't think that these history sessions are good for you, said Conn. Each time I collect you, you look distant, or worried, or both.

Contemplative, please, Conn. What is it you and David do? Hand a penny over?

Yes, that's a private joke we have – a penny for your thoughts. Mine right now are about Patrick. He has worries or pressures that he does not want to share. He hardly knows me, and I hardly know him.

What do you want to know? asked Conn. Touching the side of his nose, he warned, Don't say I told you, though.

Patrick's dad was a young boy during the Civil War here. He was wounded during some fighting and his parents decided to send him to the United States, for safety. He stayed with relatives, grew up there, and married a girl from an Irish family, and prospered. He has never been back, but is an ardent supporter of the Old Country.

Patrick is the youngest son. He became a University professor, to his father's displeasure – The bastion of the unambitious – he said. Being the ultimate wheeler-dealer capitalist, he could not see any virtue at all in academic life. Besides, Patrick was the brightest son, and he had hoped he would take over the business. Then Patrick's marriage broke up. He tried to explain to his parents that there was no hope of reconciliation. Neither could understand it. It was as simple, and as complicated as that. It was incomprehensible to two people who had been taught that family obligation always comes before love. When love has gone, family responsibility must live on. He had betrayed them both. Then, as a penance in their eyes, he said the five magic words. I will go to Ireland. An act of atonement, a return to the mother land that his father had abandoned in its time of trouble. Just before he left, he argued with his dad about Irish unification. He told him that it was not his fight. He was going to do academic research. Patrick's dad thinks that his son does not appreciate what his generation fought for; and does not understand. There is misunderstanding on both sides. A misunderstanding can be the saddest thing in the world. Patrick is a fine young man, but he carries a lot of guilt. They had reached Mrs. O'Hagan's house.

Mrs O'Hagan was curious and disturbed that Erin went out at night, alone, without David. She learned from her nephew, Kevin, that she was being tutored in Irish history by a professor. She decided that was semi-respectable. Erin could not avoid the biblical quote before she went to her room. But where shall wisdom be found; and where is the place of understanding? Job, chapter 28, verse 12. Erin thought that was an appropriate quotation.

The following evening, Patrick looked a little more refreshed. Erin was relieved. He reassured her that his exhaustion had nothing to do with their appointment, he enjoyed teaching her. He wasted no more time. He began to describe the Protestant Ascendancy.

They had the best land, jobs, privileges, and protection, for their undivided loyalty to the British Crown. The English considered them Irish, and the Irish considered them English.

They were arrogantly detached from the native population. They had fine homes. enjoyed fox-hunting, horse show week in Dublin, races at the Curragh, hunt balls, and going to London for the season. There, they had to bear the snobbery of the English aristocracy and listen to comments about their Irish ways. Although socially apart from the native Irish, they did live there, and after many generations, the Anglo-Irish Protestant had to identify with the problems there.

A group hated as much as the Ascendancy by the natives, were the so-called Castle Catholics. So named after Dublin Castle, and the favours this group looked for, there. They even showed loyalty to the British Crown, and sent sons into British military service. There was another small group, a Catholic middle class who had prospered in business. The one area not banned by the Penal Laws. Sons went to university, and daughters to convent schools. They felt secure enough not to emigrate. They had contempt, rather than hatred for the Ascendancy. They were also contemptuous towards the Irish who emigrated. American vulgarity on top of emigrant vulgarity, they said.

The Ascendancy did have a problem with finding marriagable partners. By the end of the eighteenth century, most people in Munster in the Protestant gentry, shared common ancestry.

And all the associated problems that go with inbreeding, said Erin.

There were illegitimate children fathered with local Irish girls, he continued. They took the father's name; it's an old Gaelic custom. A Catholic bishop said – Drink has done a lot of harm in Ireland, but not as much harm as the gentry.

Writers with Ascendancy backgrounds are world famous – Swift, Goldsmith, Sheridan, Burke, Wilde, Shaw, Yeats. Without these people, British theatrical history does not have much of value, from the Restoration to the Edwardians. Many of them went to England for acceptance and fame, but they did not cease to be Irish.

Oscar Wilde is a particular favourite of mine, said Erin, but I must confess that I do not know much about Jonathan Swift, a favourite of David's.

Then let's digress a little, said Patrick. Swift was a most unconventional clergyman. A rebel, dissatisfied and protesting. A restless genius, who, although a Protestant, resented English injustice in Ireland. Gulliver's Travels is not a fantasy story, it is a political satire. Swift liked Irish satiric models. He also followed the Irish tradition of the lampoon, which pretends to be flattering. The Celts believed the power of a satire or a lampoon, could actually harm you. Swift did not believe that Ireland should depend on England, or be inferior to it. The pamphlets he wrote on taxes and oppression were as powerful and as beneficial as the writings of Thomas Paine before the American Revolution. Patrick reached for a well worn notebook. I have some of Swift's sayings . . . All government without the consent of the governed is the very essence of slavery . . . We have just enough religion to make us hate, but not enough to make us love one another . . . You should think of, and deal with, every man as a villain . . . Happiness is the perpetual possession of being well deceived. Delusions and peace of mind go hand in hand.

Back to Irish history. There was a definite feeling of nationalism emerging at the end of the eighteenth century. Some of the leaders of this movement, such as Edward Fitzgerald, Smith O'Brien, Wolfe Tone, Robert Emmett, and Charles Stewart Parnell, had Ascendancy backgrounds. The French Revolution was very encouraging to the Irish. Wolfe Tone was a young Protestant lawyer, with a Catholic mother. He wanted to make Ireland a republic, along French lines, and formed the United Irishmen. He had some French support, and in December, 1796, they sailed into Bantry Bay. Bad weather prevented a landing, but the intention was made. In May, 1798, many United Irishmen were arrested, and Lord Fitzgerald was killed. A Protestant rebellion broke out in Ulster, and a Catholic one in County Wexford. French help arrived too late, in August. Wolfe Tone was captured and condemned to death. He died in prison, it is rumoured, by suicide. Tone and the French had been defeated by Lord Cornwallis of Yorktown fame. The English feared more rebellions, and decided to act. Repressively? asked Erin. Yes, and deviously, said Patrick.

The English Prime Minister, Pitt, decided to suppress the Irish Parliament because they had disagreed with his plans for union with England, with political rights for Catholics. Pitt sent over to Ireland Lord Cornwallis, the general who had surrendered at Yorktown, as the Lord-Lieutenant. Lord Castlereagh was sent as secretary. They were ordered to bring about union by buying votes and power, with a million pounds, which was added to the national debt. Pitt had seen Grattan's Parliament respond to demands from the Protestants for parliament reform, and Catholic demands for relief from the Penal Laws; and he wanted to see the Irish Parliament governed by the English Parliament, with a block of elected Irish members and Peers. Votes were purchased, as were forty-eight titles in the Irish Peerage. It was outrageous political bribery. But Pitt had promised Catholic emancipation to allow Catholics into the British Parliament, George III said, No. He believed, in that unbalanced way he had, that his coronation oath had made him a champion of Protestantism. Pitt resigned in 1801, after the legislative union of Ireland with England was introduced on January 1. Another broken promise. Catholic emancipation took a step backwards, and Protestants looked to England for stronger ties.

Strangely, Ireland was experiencing a new prosperity, economically. There was a construction boom; the Customs House and the Four Courts, date from this time. Industry and trade were moving because the Penal laws had been relaxed. With commercial growth, the Dublin slums grew. With the English betrayal, resentment festered.

Another rebellion doomed to failure took place in 1803. Led by Robert Emmett, a doctor's son, too dreamy and idealistic to be successful revolutionary. His plans went wrong, the rebellion was a shambles, he was caught and convicted. A romantic, but futile, touch to the story – Emmett was captured because he went to say goodbye to a girl, Sarah Curran. He was hanged, and became a symbol of a patriot for Ireland to remember. Many Irish people were moved by his courtroom speech – When my country takes her place among the nations of the earth, then, and not 'til then, let my epitaph be written.

So here was Ireland in the early nineteenth century. Its Parliament dissolved, legislative control transferred to England, and its economy under English control. Belfast was undergoing rapid industrialisation under Protestant control, and the rest of Ireland was England's cattle ranch.

Have you heard of Daniel O'Connell? asked Patrick.

Yes, Catholic emancipation, and Home Rule, said Erin. I don't remember details, though.

Patrick continued. He was born in 1775 and brought up in the Celtic custom of fosterage. He lived in a shepherd's cottage, with one of his uncle's tenants. As a young child he learned Irish. As a young man of eighteen, he saw Roman Catholics given the vote, and Trinity College open to them. He went to London for his legal training. As a British trained lawyer, he had a certain admiration for their constitution. As an orator, he had the power to sway large crowds. As a lawyer, he realised that open rebellion was doomed. Mass support for political, legal, and religious justice, was better.

He founded the Catholic Association, to repeal the Penal

Laws, and protect the Irish tenant farmers from absentee landlords. Out of four and a half million Catholics at this time, three quarters lived below subsistence level. He charged a penny a month membership. To illustrate the mass support that he had, this amounted to several hundred pounds a week at times. He stood for election in County Clare, and was successful. By law, he could not take his seat. As a Catholic, he would not take the oath of allegiance.

The Duke of Wellington – Dublin produced, of Ascendancy stock – was British Prime Minister. He realised that the Irish electorate would be outraged, so he recommended the passage of the Catholic Relief Bill in 1829, giving Catholics the right to hold office, and sit in parliament. The voting qualification was raised from £2 to £10, to eliminate many Catholic voters. You win a few, you lose a few, but O'Connell was playing the English at their own game – with their rules.

In 1840, he founded the National Repeal Association, to work on repealing the Union. In 1841, he became Mayor of Dublin. He was nearing seventy and he wanted to see younger men helping. In 1842, the Association was joined by three Young Irelanders – Thomas Osborne Davis, Charles Duffy and John Dillon. They had recently founded a newspaper, The Nation, which had republican views. They were young, enthusiastic and aggressive. Then came betrayal from England.

A mass rally was planned for October, 1843, at Clontarf. The British Prime Minster, Peel, cautioned O'Donnell to cancel the rally. He said it would cause bloodshed. Actually, Peel was really afraid of such a public show of strength in favour of an Irish republic. O'Connell cancelled the rally. Two hundred fifty thousand people were let down. He was then arrested and imprisoned in Richmond jail for seditious conspiracy. He had forgotten one of the rules of the English game. He was also old, tired, and sick. He was released the following September because of ill health. The Young Irelanders group broke away from the Repeal Association and ignored Daniel's plea to return. He set off on a pilgrimage to Rome in 1847, and died en route. His heart was sent to the Irish College in Rome, his body back to Dublin.

Daniel O'Connell was quite a mixture. Irish reared, English trained, able to meet the Englishman on his own grounds, on his own terms. Determined to pursue justice without rebellion, but willing to sacrifice culture for economy. He told Irish peasants that they would have to speak English if they wanted to advance economically. He had a biting tongue, he told people what he thought of them. He did not like Disraeli, they argued a lot. Daniel said that Disraeli was descended from the impenitent thief who had died upon the cross, next to the Saviour. A reference to Disraeli's Jewish background. Daniel also organised the Catholic church, through the agency of bishops and parish priests, to give it a national existence, for political purpose. He was finally devastated by the disaster of the Irish famine, which I will report on later.

What happened to the Young Irelanders? asked Erin.

They continued their militance, but a rebellion they organised for 1848 failed, because the country was in the middle of the famine. It ended in a bloody mess at Ballingarry.

Question, said Erin. O'Connell was a Catholic, but why were so many people from Protestant backgrounds involve with Irish nationalism?

Patrick smiled. They lived there, and they were part of what was happening. If your question had been: why were there not more Catholics involved? My answer would be that I believe the true Celt, although he hates the presence of foreigners, is not a convinced nationalist.

Around this same time, all sorts of political groups were forming. James Stephens, who survived the 1848 rebellion, founded the Irish Republican Brotherhood. He was known as the Fenian Chief. They gave him a mock funeral in 1848, at Kilkenny. He escaped to France. His influence helped found the Fenian Brotherhood (later, Clan na Gael) in America. I am afraid that the next muddle may have been caused by Irish-Americans. Fresh from fighting in the American Civil War, many Irishmen returned to Ireland, eager to fight. They were out of touch with the situation there. In their enthusiasm, they took control from Stephens, and the uprising of the Fenians in 1865 and 1867, failed. The Church, and other national groups, condemned the Fenians. Their plans for rebellion were interrupted by betrayal, and arrest. The Fenians however had a taste for nationalism and they continued to work towards it.

I want to talk about the Famine, before we have a break, Erin. I really could not talk about it having just had sustenance. She nodded agreement. You are too sensitive, she thought, but that is not a criticism. He continued. Since Raleigh introduced the potato to Ireland in the sixteenth century, it had become the staple crop. The potato blight that caused the crop to fail, was helped by three consecutive, wet winters; 1845, 46 and 47. Irish people were only too aware that the English who took quick, positive action, when they felt their security threatened, did not react with equal haste when Irish people were starving. Relief from private agencies appeared first. During the Famine, Irish cattle continued to be shipped out for English tables. The horror of the disease and starvation was reported by the English press. Famine struck just when the population was booming. It was estimated that a million people died. A report in an English newspaper told of unburied corpses at the roadside, eaten by hungry dogs. People taken for dead, who were buried alive. Coffins with false bottoms, for repeated use. Any natural buoyancy the Irish people may have had, was drained from them, and replaced by gloom and melancholy.

In 1840, there were eight million people in Ireland; in 1901, there were four million. In sixty years the population decreased by fifty percent, and the birthrate dropped by twenty percent. During the three years of famine, a million died and a million emigrated. The emigration continued steadily until 1914. Most went to America. Some went to Canada, Australia, and New Zealand. Because so many young people died or emigrated, an elderly population was left behind. Late marriages became a trend. The typhus and cholera that killed on land, also killed at sea. The ships arriving from Ireland were called Coffin Ships because of the number who died en route. The emigrants went from rural to urban communities and carried the trauma of that adaptation as well as the trauma of being in a new country. They took memories with them, and once established, they sent financial aid and spiritual support to Ireland. The Irish immigrants became a vocal power group that the English government could not ignore.

Patrick looked like he needed a break, so Erin suggested it. She also suppressed related questions, perceiving that it would be better to change the topic. She brought up the subject of surnames. Patrick seemed relieved at the mood change and continued to talk throughout the break.

Many Irish surnames had the O' and Mac dropped during the oppressive times of the eighteenth and nineteenth centuries. We were probably originally, O'Ryan. When there was a Gaelic revival in the early twentieth century, the prefixes were added again, by some people. Not always correctly. For example, many an O'Gorman, was previously a MacGorman. Ryan came from O'Maoilriain or O'Mulryan. It is the tenth most common name in Ireland. The Ryans were also among the earliest Irish Americans. They first went out there in 1690. He realised that break time was over and called a halt to surnames. Erin had wanted to talk personally to him but she couldn't. How could she sympathise with his personal problems and not admit that she had been prying? She had not been able to talk any further than his name.

You must remember the Land League from your history lessons in England, said Patrick.

Indeed I do, she replied. The history teacher picked on me to stand up and answer a question. What were the three F's of the Land League? I said, fuck off England, and I got a week's detention. Seriously, I have forgotten the details, she said to a much amused Patrick. He obliged.

Michael Davitt was a Fenian who spent seven years in prison as a result of an arms raid at Chester Castle. He was released in 1877, went to America for a while to promote the Fenian cause, and then returned to found the Land League in 1878. It was a legally founded organisation, and so could not be banned by the English Government. The three F's, by the way, were; fixed rents, fair rents; and the freedom to sell. The League selected estates that were notorious for rack renting, and evictions. They made life difficult for the landlord and his agent. On a Mayo estate, in 1880, they ostracised an agent called Captain Boycott; and introduced a new word to the English language. The English Government realised that this movement had mass support and they would have to react by introducing some land reforms. Gladstone was the Prime Minister at the time. He also introduced legislation to disestablish the Anglican church, as the Church of Ireland in 1869; much to the relief of the majority of Irish. The Land Reforms of 1881 were a step towards fairness for the exploited Irish tenant.

A word about Gladstone. A dour Victorian, he had in fact Celtic ancestry. His name can be traced back to the time of Malcolm III, King of Scotland. It was originally written Gledstaine. The Gaelic word gleadh means humour or tricks. (Not quite in character with William, Ewart.) Over time it was changed to Gladstones, and the Prime Minister's father dropped the s. He was, like the true Celt, concerned about the deprived and the fallen. He even tried to assist the rehabilitation of prostitutes by bringing them to his home. Mrs. Gladstone must have been understanding, as this was a most un-Victorian thing to do. He had an acute sense of social injustice, which must have affected his policies in Ireland; a reverence for the past; and unlike many prime ministers, he remained a commoner to the end.

I always think that the people are so much more interesting than the dates, in history, said Erin.

Of course they are, he replied, but I must slip the odd date in as a point of reference.

Gladstone and Disraeli see-sawed in public opinion for years, she continued, but I don't remember Disraeli concerning himself with Ireland.

No. Disraeli had a peculiar arrogance where Ireland was concerned. It was he who said, Ireland's history is a vicious cycle of bigotry and blood.

Coming from a Jew, that's an odd statement, murmured Erin.

Yes, you are right. Disraeli had experienced all sorts of discrimination. He was excluded from political office at first, because of his Jewish background. And yet he was not raised as a Jew. Maybe a man who had tried so hard to anglicise himself and deny his Jewish ancestry, could not appreciated the dilemma of the Irish people. Politically, as a Conservative, he could not show any sympathy towards Ireland. His lack of seriousness, and easy adjustment of his policies to changing conditions; made him seem to Gladstone, a time server, without conscience. Certainly O'Connell and Disraeli had many shouting matches, there was no love lost between those two.

I do not know how fair the comment, but Yeats said of Parnell and O'Connell, that they were – The great tragedian, and the great comedian, of the Irish race. Charles Stewart, Parnell's grandfather, fought against the English in 1812. The Stewarts had left Belfast for America, just before the Revolution, and they took their anti-English feelings with them. Charles himself was sent down from Cambridge, and went home to the Parnell estates in Ireland. He became a lawyer, and drifted into politics. Tim Healey said of Parnell . . . in his heart he cared little for the Irish, and had been obliged to admit that personal feeling actuated his leadership at times. He was like an Englishman in manners and speech, and did not know much about Irish tradition and culture. He hated the colour green. He was not a great public speaker. (Maybe because the platforms he spoke on were draped with green banners.)

You wouldn't be running the man down? queried Erin.

Not really, countered Patrick. I am just trying to illustrate the odd type of man that the Irish sometimes look up to as a leader.

Back to history. Parnell allied with Michael Davitt. They formed the New Departure, and were both arrested and imprisoned. Parnell replaced Isaac Butt as head of the Home Rule Party in 1878. His authority was absolute for the next twelve years. He did not want an armed revolution, or a compromised settlement, like Butt. He would work on constitutional means, the way the English play the game. He and Davitt and Gladstone worked together. The Irish members in Westminster played a power role now, especially when there was a minority government. Parnell made it clear that he wanted the Act of Union abolished, and replaced by Irish Home Rule. Gladstone introduced a Home Rule Bill that was defeated by thirty votes, in 1886. A section of his Liberal Party had sided with the Conservatives to defeat it. There was heavy opposition from the Ulster Unionist members. Then, just when things were underway again, a scandal obliterated Home Rule for a while. In 1889, Captain W.O'Shea, a former M.P. for an Irish constituency, and friend of Joseph Chamberlain, English Tory leader, sued his wife, Kitty, for divorce. Parnell was cited as co-respondent, and he did not contest the petition. It was an English plot to undermine Parnell's successes, and it worked. The O'Sheas had been apart for years without the bother of a formal divorce, the timing was convenient for the English government. Parnell would not resign from the Party, although the morally outraged population demanded it. A strange attitude, the Irish have towards divorce. All other Catholic countries in Europe now have divorce laws, but still the Irish hold out.

Erin saw an opportune moment to speak up, but it passed. Patrick continued, . . . Parnell's Party suffered defeats in by-elections, so he went to England with Kitty. He married her. He died in Brighton, a broken man, in October 1891. Thousands turned out for his funeral in Dublin, as if death had cleared his name. The Fenian Chief, James Stephens, laid a wreath on his grave.

Gladstone introduced a second Home Rule Bill in 1892. The Commons passed it, but the House of Lords would not. Too many of them had acquaintances who held land in Ireland, as absentee landlords. Gladstone retired in 1894 and died four years later. The Tories, in power from 1896-1906, did nothing to promote an independent Ireland. Ireland was used as a pawn in the fight between English Liberals and Tories.

The eighteen nineties in Ireland was a time of cultural activity. There was a literary revival. Sir Samuel Ferguson, poet and antiquarian, and Standish James O'Grady, both from Protestant backgrounds, wrote about Celtic Ireland. They inspired W.B. Yeats and George Russell, when they produced their works. Douglas Hyde, also from a Protestant background, rejected the English language as unsuitable for Irish national literature. He believed that the Celtic heritage could only be appreciated in the Irish tongue. He was the first president of the Gaelic League, founded in 1893 to promote the revival of Gaelic. The Irish National Literary Society and the Abbey Theatre were founded by Yeats and Lady Gregory.

The Gaelic Athletic Association, founded in 1884, revived traditional Irish games.

We are getting there aren't we? asked Erin.

Indeed we are, said Patrick, but now a lot happens in a short period of time.

Don't skip anything, she said.

Between 1891-1914, the English government policies helped social and economic improvements but nothing was done for Home Rule. A Home Rule Bill introduced in 1912, suffered the same fate as an earlier one; passed by the Commons, not by the Lords. In June, a Liberal M.P., Agar Robartes, moved an amendment to the Home Rule Bill, proposing the exclusion of the Ulster Counties – Antrim, Armagh, Down, and Londonderry. Redmond opposed it saying – The idea of two nations in Ireland, is revolting and hateful. The reason that the Home Rule Bill has been resurrected at all was that the Liberals had a minority government and needed Irish Parliamentary support.

How many times can this bill be shelved? asked Erin.

The third one was passed, but its implementation was delayed because of the beginning of World War I. Ulster Protestants were anxious, and held a Covenant Day, declaring loyalty to the British Crown. Then the king interfered. George V learned that 57 officers at the Curragh said that they would resign rather than coerce Ulster. He instructed the prime minister to exclude Ulster from the Bill. It was so done.

In 1885, when Home Rule seemed possible, Protestants in Ulster had formed the Unionist Party at an Orange Order meeting. In 1910, Edward Carson became their leader. the son of a Presbyterian architect, he had studied law at Trinity College, and became a member of both English and Irish bars. He successfully defended Lord Queensbury against Oscar Wilde, in the libel action of 1895. Oscar Wilde said of him . . . no doubt he will perform his task with the added bitterness of an old friend. In 1892, he had become Irish Solicitor General, and was elected to parliament. He organised an armed volunteer force to defend Ulster, and kept it legal by applying to Belfast magistrates for authorisation to train men with arms. By 1911, there were 100,000 men enlisted. In 1913, in Belfast, Carson set up an illegal provisional government. People in the south were becoming alarmed about the militance in the north. In 1913, Eoin Macneil suggested that a volunteer force be assembled, for defence. By 1914, the Irish Volunteers, under Redmond, numbered 200,000. They would break up the same year. The English government banned the importation of arms to Ireland. Winston Churchill's father, Lord Randolph, gave the north their slogan – Ulster will fight, and Ulster will be right.

Syphilitic old fool, murmured Erin. Patrick smiled.

On instructions from George V, a conference was called at Buckingham Palace, in July 1914. Redmond and Dillon, represented the Home Rule Party; Ulster Unionists were represented by Carson and Craig; Landsdowne and Bonar Law, represented the English Conservatives; Asquith and Lloyd George, the Liberals. After four days the discussions broke down; they were unable to agree. The Bill was amended anyway, to exclude Ulster.

When the First World war broke out, John Redmond had promised England the support of his southern Volunteer forces. Republican and Sinn Fein elements objected, they broke away with 12,000 men to form the Irish Volunteers, under Macneil and Pearse. Redmond's group called themselves the National Volunteers and fought for England. The Ulster Volunteers did too; but it was well know that within the British Army, preferential treatment was given to the Ulster force.

Redmond was a fool, said Erin.

I think that we have a militant nationalist here he said. Time for some definitions; some say that a Unionist is an Irishman who believes that he is as English as an Englishman; a Loyalist is an Irishman who believes that he is more English than an Englishman: a Nationalist has an irrational love for his country; and a Patriot will prove that love by fighting.

The conversational digression had broken the historical thread. They paused for breaktime. It was getting late, but the intention was to finish that evening. Over cocoa, Patrick said that the struggle in Ireland at that time had come to the attention of Lenin. He was impressed with the formation of a Citizen's Army, by a group of working-class men, under James Connolly. They did this after a strike and lockout, in Dublin.

History resumed. The Rising. It was a bit of a shambles. The timing was because of English preoccupation with the War. In January, 1916, it was decided that Easter Sunday would be a suitable date because it was followed by a holiday Monday. People would not miss a work day to join a revolution.

I would have thought it would have been the other way round, she said, people would not want to give up a holiday to join a revolution, bugger the workday.

Erin, you should have been there to help them plan it.

A few words about Padraig Pearse, one of the planners. The son of an English gravestone decorator, who moved to Ireland, Pearse was educated by the Christian Brothers, and became a lawyer. He was interested in the Celts; their mythology and their custom of child fosterage as a means of education. In 1908, he left the legal profession, and opened a boys' school, called St. Enda's. Celtic studies were an important part of the curriculum. Some of the students had said that it wasn't much fun telling fantastic lies to Mr. Pearse, because he believed them. His was a strange background for a revolutionary leader, but he did inspire the men who fought.

Back to the Rising. It actually took place on Easter Monday, 1916, after orders were changed. Instead of a nationwide uprising, it only took place in Dublin and locally. The military Council of the Irish Republican Brotherhood made the final arrangements. Only 2,000 of a possible 10,000 Volunteers showed up, plus Connolly's army of 200. A shipload of arms from Germany was scuttled, after the English spotted the boat. Roger Casement, put ashore in Tralee by a German submarine, was arrested. He was eventually tried and executed for treason.

Back to the Rising, again. On that Monday, most of Dublin went out for the day. When they returned, many of the civilian population were angry at the rebels, and shouted at them in the streets. Pearse read the Proclamation of the Republic to a group of Dubliners, many of whom did not know what was happening. Twenty Volunteers went to Dublin Castle, shot the one man on duty there, and left. The Military Council, led by Pearse and

Connolly, made their headquarters in the General Post Office building on Sackville Street, now called O'Connell Street. Sean T. O'Coellaigh took a cart around the streets and gave out information about the new republic, on hand-bills.

I see what you mean about shambles, she said. If only all revolutions had such a low profile!

British troops coming into Dublin to fight the rebels were puzzled that some residents were cheering them, not aware of the revolution in their midst. An English gunboat fired on the Post Office from the River Liffey, and set it on fire. Four hundred fifty rebels and 103 English soldiers were killed. On Saturday, Pearse signed an unconditional surrender, and the rebellion was over. Fourteen of the leaders were shot, including the seven who signed the Proclamation of the Republic. The deaths of Pearse, Connolly, Clarke, and the others filled the population with patriotic remorse. Now they had their support. Seventy five others involved were given life sentences, including Eamonn De Valera. In December, 1916, he and others were released, partly to satisfy America, who was about to enter the War. The executed rebels had become heroes overnight. Dillon warned Prime Minister Asquith in a letter – You are letting loose a river of blood . . . between two races, who, after 300 years of hatred and strife, we had nearly succeeded in bringing together. Between July 1917, and April 1918, all parties involved tried to work out a solution, nothing happened. The English Government had a new group to reckon with, Sinn Fein.

This political party was founded in 1905, by Arthur Griffith. In 1918, England tried to introduce compulsory military service to Ireland. The law was passed but not enforced. The Irish were furious. The Sinn Fein, determined to gain political strength, ran their candidates in the election. Michael Collins, who I will tell you about later, went through the list, and eliminated all moderates. Before the election, seventy people were imprisoned. Thomas Ashe died while on a hunger strike in Mountjoy prison. He had a hero's funeral. the election of December, 1918, produced 73 successful Sinn Fein candidates, 34 were in prison. De Valera defeated Dillon in East Mayo and the Sinn Fein replaced the Home Rulers as the dominant political party.

They set up their own Republican Parliament, the Dail Eireann at the Mansion House, in Dublin, on January 21, 1919. De Valera was elected the president in April; in September, the English declared the Dail illegal, and they went underground.

Time out for De Valera. Born in New York, in 1882, to a Spanish father and an Irish mother, he moved to Ireland to be reared by relatives in 1885, when his father died. He joined the Gaelic League, married a teacher he met there, and joined the Irish Republican Brotherhood in 1914. He was an intellectual revolutionary, and although he joined the 1916 Rising, he thought that it should have been cancelled. He was a hard, practical, publicly humourless man, but he dominated politics for fifty years, with only a short break. His type of authoritarianism appealed to the Irish public, who respected, rather than loved him. Dev himself realised the cynicism of the Irish towards politicians. He said, In England you can say anything, as long as you do the right thing; in Ireland, you can do anything as long as you say the right thing.

He did have a sense of humour, she said.

While we are talking about people, rather than events, a few words about Michael Collins. Born in 1890, at Klonakilty, County Cork, the name Collins anglicised from the Irish Cullane (O Coileain). He went to England to work as a postal clerk, and returned in 1916, just in time to join the Rising. He was one of 200 rebels imprisoned in Wales for six months. He was not an intellectual revolutionary; he had one aim, Irish independence. Where the Irish respected Dev with their minds; they loved Collins with their hearts. He could be violently impulsive and ruthless in his methods, when necessary. His men called him – the big fellow –. Not meaning his height of five foot ten, but his character. He was Minister of Finance in the outlawed Dail. £10,000 was offered for information leading to his arrest. He moved around openly, confident that his fellow Irish would not turn him in. He was involved in two and a half years of guerrilla warfare; he was an expert. The guerrillas became known as the Irish Republican Army.

In March, 1920, the Black and Tans arrived. They were hardened, British, ex-servicemen, unemployed, and given ten shillings a day and all they could steal. Their name came from their uniform, half military, and half police colours. They used ruthless tactics against the rebels, with full permission. Their reprisals were shocking. They were hated for their methods. If they were fired on by the I.R.A. whole towns nearby were burned. Along with the Royal Irish Constabulary, British forces were 43,000. There were about 15,000 rebels. The entire business section of Cork was burned to the ground, firemen were not allowed near the flames. The Mayor of Cork was imprisoned. Terence MacSwiney died in jail in 1920, after a hunger strike of 75 days. He became a symbol of Ireland's determination to resist English control.

Collins had set up a very good spy network. He knew the danger caused by informers, he wanted tight control. As a result, the British brought in the Cairo Group – 16 officers, trained in intelligence, in Egypt. Collins' men executed 14 of them. As a result, the British sent Black and Tans and Auxiliaries to Croke Park, where a Gaelic football game was in progress. They fired on the spectators and players, without warning, killing 14, and wounded 60. Three I.R.A. men captured in a hotel, were questioned, tortured, and shot. No trial.

Who was responsible for issuing those orders to shoot on civilians? she asked.

Who knows? he replied. Ultimately, the British government.

In the 1920 election, Sinn Fein won every seat in the south, except Trinity College. In the north, the Unionists had the majority. In Dublin, the second Dail sat.

Although Welsh born, and an early supporter of Home Rule, Lloyd George, the British Prime Minister, did not like the south. Dev met with him in 1921, and was asked for a translation of the words *saorstat Eireann* and gave the meaning Free State. Dev was then asked the Irish word for republic, and they had some debate about it. Lloyd George concluded: Must we not admit that the Celts were never republicans, and have no native word for the idea.

Devious old sod, she said.

That is not objective, Erin. I know, you are the one who is supposed to be objective, I can say what I like. Anyway, Lloyd George was responsible for the Articles of Agreement, whereby Ireland would be known as the Free State, that is the southern half.

Ulster would remain apart, with its own parliament. It was said she could opt to join the Fee State if she wished, but of course this option was not taken. The Dail of December 3 decided on extreme changes to these Articles, and delegates were sent to London. Dev did not go, and this was a costly mistake. Griffith and Collins were sent as delegates. Lloyd George used the same deceptive tactics on them that Peel had used on O'Connell. He threatened more violence and bloodshed, if the treaty was not signed. It was signed on December 6, 1921. An oath of allegiance to the Crown was accepted; control by British forces of certain ports in peacetime; unlimited control in wartime; the parliament of southern Ireland would be that of the Irish Free State. A boundary Commission was supposed to review the six northern Counties, and possible amalgamation with the south, but this never materialised.

On December 7, one day later, the Unionists exercised their option to stay out of the Free State, and declared Northern Ireland a province of Britain. The newly formed Constabulary quickly added 60,000 auxiliaries in case of retaliation by the thirty percent Catholic population.

De Valera was furious, but it was too late to change the agreements. In January 1922, the Treaty was approved by a divided Dail, by 64-57 votes. Dev resigned, and Griffith took his place. The Government was split into Pro-Treaty, and Anti-Treaty forces. Collins headed the Provisional Government, which was Anti-Treaty, and Griffith headed the Dail, which was Pro-Treaty. The general population wanted a peaceful solution, and elected a Pro-Treaty majority that June. Lloyd George put pressure on Arthur Griffith to protect the Treaty, and break with the Republicans. On June 22, Free State troops fired on Republican troops in the Four Courts in Dublin, Civil War had begun. This was particularly sad, after all the deception, he said, to end up this way. It is of special significance to me. My father as a young boy got involved with the fighting on the Anti-Treaty side. His parents sent him to relatives in the States, to recover after he was wounded. Erin saw an opening for a personal talk, but the time was wrong. It was late, and he wanted to finish.

By the end of thc summer, Free State forces held all main

cities, and most of the country. The Catholic hierarchy, which supported Sinn Fein in 1918, now called for their excommunication. Collins became an armed fugitive, never spending more than two nights in the same place. On August 12 he heard that the fifty year old Griffith had died from a stroke. Not long after, the thirty-two year old Collins died in an ambush, on a road in County Cork, standing his ground and firing at the assailants.

On December 6, 1922, the first anniversary of the signing of the Treaty, the Irish Free State came into existence. The first Governor General was Tim Healey, a Home Rule politician. Violence continued between the two sides, and the Republicans, sensing a loss, destroyed a lot of property. The war was costly, economically and socially. By March, 1923, De Valera was ready to talk peace. He agreed to a Republican surrender, and waived his own demands. Republican hold-outs were hunted down, and there were reprisal executions, during which Erskine Childers, and many others, were killed. The Irish were ashamed of their brutality to one another.

The first Free State government under William Cosgrave had to cope with bitter and disillusioned people, at the end of the war, in May, 1923. The Free State reluctantly endorsed the partition of Ireland, in 1924, losing the six northern states. What about revenge after the revolution? asked Erin. It never happened. Protestants never suffered wholesale massacre as the losers did in other European revolutions. Those who chose to, could leave the country.

In the north, Unionists did not want to give Catholics a fair deal, economically. They wanted to continue the tradition of Catholic suppression. Ulster ended proportional representation, and began gerrymandering. In 1922 the government passed the Special Powers Act, which gave authorities the power to arrest anyone, without a warrant, on suspicion of, . . . acting, or having acted, or of being about to act in a manner prejudicial to the state . . . People could be held for indefinite periods without charge, or trial. This Act would later become a model for fascist governments in Europe. It was renewed annually, and became permanent in 1933.

Where was British democracy hiding?

De Valera, in prison for a year, created a new party in 1926, from Republicans who shared his ideals. They were called Fianna Fail (Soldiers of Destiny).

By 1932, Fianna Fail defeated Fine Gael (Tribe of Gaels) and there was a unique situation, where the losers of the Civil War formed the government. Fianna Fail cancelled land annuities to Britain, abolished the Governor General in favour of a President, abolished the oath to the Crown, and renamed the Free State, Eire. As part of the Eire Constitution of 1937, the British monarchy was excluded from any sovereignty in Ireland and Catholicism and given legal recognition as the majority religion.

We seem to be getting there, she said.

How about the next few years in the new few minutes? he asked. Conn had already called for Erin, and was due back.

Britain retaliated with an economic war. Trade barriers were erected. It did not last. The British naval bases were relinquished. The I.R.A. fell out with De Valera. The Second World War was on the horizon. In a move to keep Eire neutral, Dev outlawed the I.R.A. The Catholics in Ulster, looked to the I.R.A. for support in a Protestant dominant government and community. The rest is recent history.

As Conn isn't back, I have a story about the proclaiming of the Republic in 1949. The story goes that the Prime Minister, John A. Costello, went to a conference in Canada. The Governor General there was Earl Alexander of Tunis of northern Irish Protestant origin. At a social function, he made a point of ignoring Costello. Costello called a press conference and announced that the south would be an independent republic, breaking all ties with the Commonwealth, and Northern Ireland. The Republic of Ireland was conceived in haste, that afternoon. And in haste, I must go. There is a taxi outside.

Patrick hugged her. We must talk again, Erin. Not history, just talk.

Good, it has been very difficult for me to keep my mouth shut. I am naturally talkative, she said. But the topic was fascinating, so I disciplined myself. I should ask a friend of mine to give you an account with a different slant, said Patrick. Is he good looking? she asked. I must go, Conn is looking patient, which actually means he is seething. I copied this quote from Roger Casement, in the library yesterday. She pressed a piece of paper into Patrick's hand.

Ireland has suffered at the hands of British administrators, a more prolonged series of evils, deliberately inflicted, than any other community of civilised men.

When he looked up, she had gone. Patrick bit his lip. My father would have been so pleased to have had her as a son.

Chapter
THREE

The next day Conn collected Erin in his taxi.

How was the history lesson last night? It was too late for us to talk.

It was exhilarating, confusing and disgusting.

Nice choice of adjectives, he said.

There was a lot to learn, and it had to be diffused quickly, but I tried to do some reading at the library between lessons. A quote I saw by Thomas O'Hagan really summed up the frustration I felt when I heard the history of this country. He said, What Irish genius might have done, had it not beaten its wounded and bleeding wings against the iron bars of oppression, we know not.

It seems that it was up to the emigrants to show what Irish genius could do, commented Conn.

Erin continued, I was struck by the futility of so much betrayal and failed rebellion. It made me angry and confused.

Yes, said Conn, if you are not confused you haven't really understood the situation.

The English literary effort to assuage their guilt regarding intrusion in India hasn't been complemented with similar efforts about their intrusion here, she noted.

Haven't you read A Passage to Ireland and The Jewel in the Harp? asked Conn.

Erin chuckled. What about Celts, by Conn, she said.

Well it has to be a mobile education, I can't have you round to my place in the evenings, like Patrick. I have my reputation to consider. I might sound a little book like from time to time, but I promise I won't give you chronological constipation. And don't you worry about taking up my time. Erin. Whoever made time, made plenty of it!

Being in a taxi with Conn was like being with a tornado in a bottle, it was like trying to grab running water. Trying to see air. His mouth frequently ran ahead of his brain. Topics were changed in mid sentence. Universal theories diffused: philosophies, confounded. It was difficult to keep up, to follow the thought track, and to remain just one step behind. It was the impact of the glimpse. It was harrowing, frustrating, challenging, but never dull.

Where would you like to begin?

With the name. When Patrick spoke of the basketball team he pronounced the C as an S. I pronounce it like a K.

It depends whether you have Greek or Roman sympathies. The Greeks called them Keltoi and the Romans, Celtae. Take your choice, hard C or soft C. It doesn't matter, it's not the name we are after, it's the substance. We have no written records from the Celts, we have to rely on contemporary Greek and Roman accounts; biased as they no doubt were.

That lady, said Conn pointing through the window, has not heard of The Third Law of Force. A woman was struggling to put up her umbrella; the victim of a sudden shower.

Well, what is it? Erin asked.

The Third Law states: Don't force it, get a large hammer, winked Conn. The showers forced passengers into the taxi and they usually chatted, so the Celts were abandoned for a while. When the showers stopped, the thread of his thoughts continued.

The accounts we have from the Greeks and Romans were about the Celts in Gaul, mostly. The Greek Strabo said that; They were wildly fond of war. He also tells us that, They try not to become stout and fat bellied. Any young man who exceeds the standard length of girdle, has to pay a fine. Combat, described by a Greek historian, writing in the first century, B.C. When two armies are face to face, swords drawn and spears couched, the Celtic poets throw themselves into the midst of the combat and appease the warriors as though they were charming wild beasts. Even among the most savage barbarians, anger submits to the rule of wisdom and the god of war pays homage to the muses. Don't think, however, that they weren't fierce and barbaric in war. Siculus said, They cut the heads off enemies and attach them to the necks of their horses.

Greek scholars from Alexandria in the second century A.D. believed Druids to be moral philosophers because they promoted the immortality of the soul. They believed them to be truly religious men, concerned with the study of nature and enjoyment of a close relationship with the gods. The Romans were hypocritical in their observations. They criticised Celtic sacrifices while conveniently forgetting their own barbaric customs. Lucan, a Roman writing in the first century A.D., describes three Celtic gods and their sacrificial ceremonies . . . Cruel Teutates propitiated by bloody sacrifices; uncouth Esus of the barbarous altars; and Taranis, whose altar is not more benign than that of the Scythian, Diana. It was said that people sacrificed to Taranis were burned, sometimes in groups, inside wooden cages. Victims of Teutates were asphyxiated by being plunged headfirst into a vat; and sacrifices to Esus were hung from trees and wounded ritually.

How picturesque, I wonder where these customs originated? asked Erin.

Not very pleasant, said Conn, but the Romans had some of their own inventive ways of killing people that were equally brutal. Yes, I believe that someone being torn apart by a lion is not a pretty sight. Back to more spiritual matters. It was Lucan who reported the Celtic belief that after death, the soul controlled the body in another world, which transcended time and space.

A little nearer to home, the Romans historian, Tacitus, described Celtic battle preparations in Anglesey. The women were in black and running wildly among the warrious, like Furies. They held flaming torches and had untidy hair. The Druids, in white robes, were also with the warriors. They were lifting up their hands to heaven and shouting horrible incantations. Actually, the Roman war machine beat the Celts at this particular battle, but they were much impressed with the pre-battle frenzy, as well as the heroic fighting of the warriors. Caesar wanted to eliminate the Druids. He believed that they were behind the Celtic aggressiveness. He said that they were itinerant priests, moving from tribe to tribe, exempt from paying taxes or bearing arms. Membership was exclusive and only men of intellect were accepted. Their training was done in secret, and could be as long as twenty years. Pliny, who visited Gaul in the first century A.D. said that the name Druid was probably from the Greek word for oak-*drus*. This tree was sacred to the Celts. He also witnessed a Druid ceremony . . . on the sixth day of the waxing moon, at the base of an old oak, with a rare growth of mistletoe, a Druid climbed the tree holding a golden sickle. He cut a sprig of mistletoe, which dropped into a white cloth, held by two assistants. Two white bulls were then sacrificed to an un-named deity . . .

Romans had some interesting comments on Celtic women. Ammianus Marcellinus said; A Gallic woman fighting beside her man is a match for a whole troop of foreigners. Steely-eyed, she swells her neck, gnashes her teeth, flexes her huge white biceps, and rains wallops and kicks as though from the twisted cords of a catapult. Dio Cassius recorded the reply of a Celtic woman who was accused of being morally loose by a Roman woman . . . We fulfil the demands of nature in a much better way than you Roman women. We consort openly with the best men, whereas you allow yourselves to be debauched in private, by the vilest . . . That was letting the Roman woman know who was the more liberated and civilised, winked Conn. You know that the Romans did not conquer Ireland physically, though the General Agricola, boasted that Ireland could be taken and held by one legion and a few auxiliaries. What they didn't do physically, they did spiritually, later. But that is Michael's territory. Enough of these classical quotes.

They're off, yelled Conn. The taxi had stopped at a red light to allow walkers to weave and wind their way across the street. Conn was taking loud bets with himself as to who would be the winner. Who would reach the other side first. The filly in brown boots and green raincoat got away fast at the light. She has to post a large, brown envelope and is in a hurry. But wait, coming up fast on the outside, the colt in the tweed jacket has broken into a gallop, he's edging ahead of her steady trot. Yes, yes, no! The filly's brown boot tipped the curb opposite one second ahead of the colt's black lace-ups. The filly has it, whooped Conn. This little racing ritual was to occur frequently and eventually Erin learned to pick a pedestrian, and place a bet.

Do you remember, Conn, when a woman jockey won the Irish Grand National and nobody cheered? The commentator said that the silence was deafening. That was because the horse was an outsider, said Conn. Back to the Celts.

They were never a nation politically speaking. They were tribally linked by culture, religion, and language. At their peak they could be found from the Atlantic to the Black Sea, and from the Mediterranean to the North Sea. Between 800 and 500 B.C. we call their culture, Hallstatt, named after archaeological finds near present day Salzburg. Between 500 and 50 B.C. the culture was called La Téne after a site discovered on Lake Neûchatel. As to their racial origins, it is thought that they were Indo-European, and may have come from east of the Carpathian mountains. Sorry to be so vague, but the cunning Celts left no written records in a perverse attempt to make life difficult for historians.

Around 800 B.C. they began to migrate, and introduce their iron working techniques to the rest of Europe. The Scythians from the Steppe region probably introduced the Celts to their cavalry technique with horses, and the wearing of trousers for riding. Celts introduced to Europe the use of iron for tools and weapons, agriculture and transport. We can track their spread a little, by ancient place names. *Nemeton* was a sacred place, *briga*, was a hill, and *dunum* was a fort. From that we get Dundee and Verdun. Tribal names have given us Rheims from the *Remi* tribe: Chartres from the *Carnutes*; Paris from the *Parisii*; Bologna and Bohemia, from the *Boii*; Belgium from the *Belgae*; Helvetica from the *Helvetii*; and Britain from the *Brythons*.

The Romans called them *Galli* and from that we get the old name for France, *Gaul*; *Galicia*, in Spain, Poland and the western Ukraine; and *Galatia* in Asia-Minor. We know that there were Celtic settlements in Lyons, Geneva, Strasbourg, Bonn, Vienna, Belgrade, Budapest, Ankara and London. There are European rivers with Celtic names; the Seine, Rhine, Danube, Shannon and Thames. Speaking of rivers, it's time for some liquid refreshment;

that guided tour of Celtic Europe has made me quite dry. The taxi pulled up outside one of Conn's locals.

The regulars were relaxing over a lengthy lunch. They were comparing notes on the effort of doing nothing; and then taking a rest afterwards. Being idle is not doing nothing; it is the freedom to do anything. Sure, joined in Conn, you need a strong sense of personal identity to be idle. Socrates, joined in another voice, said that; He is not only idle that does nothing, but he is also idle who might be better employed. We'll drink to that. The conversation turned to married life. They seemed to forget Erin was there, because, as she reminded herself, she kept her mouth shut.

The only thing that I have in common with my wife is that we got married on the same day. Don't marry for money, you can borrow it cheaper. Hey you know, monogamy leaves a lot to be desired. I can't think of anything that marriage can give me, said a bachelor, but I can think of plenty of things that it could take away. Look at Conn, here, he wouldn't marry. He's old enough to know better. No man, replied Conn, is old enough to know better. Why didn't you marry then?

Because I would want to be married and not divorced or trapped. It isn't marriage that fails, it's people that fail. To make marriage work, you have to work at it. I am used to my own company and I know that I would find it hard to make concessions to anyone else.

I heard that she wouldn't have you! We all have to settle for what we can; life is one long compromise. What man or woman achieves eternal bliss with the partner of their choice? A voice from the perimeter chimed in. Will Rogers said that; Marriage isn't a word, it's a sentence. Laughter erupted and flowed over the words to quench the serious tones. Conn's not the type of man who would clamber over ten naked women to get to a bottle of beer. I would, somebody yelled.

Erin sat quietly while the anti-female comments flew. Conn gestured that it was time to go, and a member of the chorus realised that she was with him. Well, now little lady, you're the quiet one.

Erin's cheeks dimpled demurely. She spoke to the group.

Women's faults are many, but men have only two. Everything they say and everything they do. There was a slight pause then joint laughter. They returned to the taxi.

Any questions – about the Celts?

Yes, what about Celtic place names closer to home?

Cymry was the Celtic name for the Welsh; and Cymbria turned into Cumbria.

Where did Wales come from?

From the Saxon word *Wallas*, meaning foreigner. The same word gave Cornwall its name. But Cornwall survived as the Celtic kingdom of Dumnonia until the ninth century A.D. The Celtic prefix tref, or tre, meaning village, predominates the Saxon suffix ton – for settlement in Cornwall. The Calder valley, along the Pennine Way, was once the centre of Elmet, the last Celtic kingdom in Yorkshire. It stretched as far north as Craven, and as far south as Leeds. Both Celtic names.

In 43 A.D. the Romans came and Celtic Britons were driven to the corners. The northwest, far north and far west. People in Wales, Cornwall, north and northwest England, the Isle of Man and the Channel Isles still have a strong Celtic flavour. The machine of the legion was no match for tribal warriors and the Celts succumbed. Boadicea, or Boudicca, was one of these tough, heroic, Celtic women. She fought back after Roman treachery and rape had violated her tribe, in East Anglia. But the Celtic population had to assimilate, or flee. Only in Ireland did they remain, undisturbed, until the ninth century A.D. Here, their culture flourished.

In Ireland, the Celtic language was Gaelg. In Scotland and the Isle of Man it was Gaelic – from Goidelic. Welsh, Cornish, and the Breton language came from Brythonic. There was a European Celtic language called Gaulish. but it died out when the Romans conquered Gaul, in one A.D. Gaelic, as it is mostly called now, is a beautiful language. It is diverse, and lends itself to eloquence, poetry, and expressiveness. It has twice the number of sounds of other European languages. It loses much of its charm in translation. The saying, to mind your P's and Q's, comes from the Celtic language structure. In Ireland, Highland Scotland, and the Isle of

Man there is a Q sound, now written as a C. The language from Wales, Brittany and Cornwall, has a P sound. The word for son in Welsh is, map, sometimes shortened to, ap. In Ireland and Scotland, son is mac, sometimes shortened to mc. I think of the MaC, Mac, Mc, mac, names as the Celtic revenge. Have you looked them up in the telephone book; it's murder!

Their laughs dwindled down to smiles, as two youths defiantly wandered in front of the taxi. These are difficult times for the young, said Conn. If it's not these notice-me hairstyles and clothes, then it's the standardised uniform of brand name jeans and shoes. I have seen the glassy-eyed look of kids so spaced out on drugs that they don't even remember where they live. Can things be so good, or so bad that they feel the need to do this to themselves?

Celtic warriors in preparation for battle washed their hair in lime and put it into stiff spikes to dry. But they were trying to look fierce and scare their opponents. They also rushed into battle, naked. They believed that it gave them magical protection. No clothes, just maybe a torque around their neck, or an amulet. Of course, they were not protected from death by their nakedness; but it must have given the other side a momentary disadvantage! There is a fine statue from the first century B.C. called The Dying Gaul. It shows a naked warrior, sitting as he approaches death. He wears a torque around his neck. It was to commemorate the win of the king of Pergamon over the Galatians of Asia-Minor. It is touching and beautiful. I saw it in the Capitoline Museum in Rome.

The king of Bithinia, in the third century B.C. invited 20,000 Celtic warriors to present day Turkey. After years of fighting and eventual defeat at Pergamon in 230 B.C., these mercenaries eventually settled in Galatia and became early Christian converts. Remember Paul's Epistle to the Galatians?

Celts plundered the shrine at Delphi in 279 B.C. and moved north to Thrace. Some stayed and settled, but were attacked by the Thracians. Celts captured Rome in 387 B.C. but they didn't say. They preferred it further north, and some remained in the Po valley. However, they were beaten by the Romans in 225 B.C. at the battle of Telamon. In Spain, Celts were settling in the north; in the region known as Galacia. In central Spain, they inter-married with Iberians to produce Celtiberians. They withstood Roman occupation for two hundred years.

Then the Roman war machine started to roll. For some reason Caesar decided to crush the Gallic area and leave the Germanic area alone. Culturally the two were connected. After many years of fighting, Caesar finally defeated the Celtic warriors, and their leader Vercingetorix in 52 B.C. at Alesia. Then the Romans headed for Britain. Some of the displaced Celts there went to Ireland. There had been two other waves of Celtic immigration to Ireland, in the third and fifth centuries B.C. When the Celts arrived there they found an established culture, as Patrick must have told you. What did you think of him? It was time to change the topic.

Erin reiterated that she had found Patrick charming, thoughtful, and polite. Yes, I like Americans, said Conn. They are good passengers and tip well. But in return they like to be appreciated. They glow when you say something positive about their country. The young ones though – they like to hear more. They ask me what I don't like. So I tell them that I don't like a materialistic society where satisfaction and happiness are elusive goals. I tell them that looking for money and new experiences has driven them to tranquillisers, drugs and discontent. Then I tell them that the disease has crept into Western Europe, and even into Ireland. I tell them that in a materialistic society you are ranked on how successful you appear to be. Whether you have made it; or will make it soon. Living always for goals and for the future; life is a state of becoming, not being. Life can be fractured by excessive demands. Materialists do not know what to do with their inner selves. By this time they look so distraught that I have to lighten things up a bit. I tell them that they have great potential, and it is up to them how to use it. I tell them that I like the HOWTO . . . books that they have, especially the ones about sex. Was there ever a people who talked about it more, and enjoyed it less?

Erin tried to steer him back to the course topic. Well, that's the American psyche, what about the Celts?

Rumour has it, he said, that the were: argumentative, boastful, chivalrous, controversial, courageous, honourable, imaginative, impetuous, individualistic, moody, poetic, passionate, proud, spontaneous, talkative, tenacious, and versatile. Are you sorry you asked? They had a great respect for learning and used fosterage as a method of education. They believed that by diligent study, a man could rise above the status of his birth. They loved the arts, respected nature, and had a strong sense of justice and family honour. What were their weaknesses? They were wildly fond of alcohol and they loved a good fight. They were tribal and had no nationalistic, centralised government. Because of this they were able to be conquered. They looked to the tribe and their family, they founded no empires. Nationalism and state bureaucracy were not Celtic inventions. If you look for a Celt, look for an attitude and a cultural foundation.

They had kings, though, and High Kings – Patrick told me, said Erin. Ard Ri. Sure, and King Arthur and all that lot were modelled on a Celtic Ard Ri, he replied. Did Patrick tell you about Dalriada? Before she could answer, he was off on a digression . . . The famine in Munster, about 200 A.D., forced a family called Riada to try their luck in Argyll. They named their settlement there Dalriada – Riada's place. There was a Dalriada in Antrim and three brothers from there decided to go over to Argyll. In 504 A.D. Fergus, Angus and Lorne left for the other Dalriada. Fergus became king. When his grandson, Conall, died in 574 A.D.; Aidan, his son, was made king. He was the first Christian king and he declared Scottish Dalriada to be independent from Ireland. He was crowned on the Stone of Scone – now in Westminster Abbey – which his great-grandfather, Fergus, had brought over from Ireland. In 842 A.D. Kenneth McAlpin united the Picts and Scots; and the heirs of this Dalriada king ruled until 1285. Then the ancient Irish bloodline passed through a maternal line to the Stuarts. The original Dalriadans were Scots from Scotia; an old name for Ireland. Scotland was actually called Alba until the tenth century A.D. when it became Scotland. That reminds me . . . the old Celtic name for Brittany was Armorica . . . now doesn't that sound like America? I'm dry, let's take some liquid refreshment. Erin noticed that they did not stop at the same pub as the previous day.

Over lunch they talked of Scottish Highland clans and their

allegiance to their chieftain; very tribal, very Celtic. A Saxon princess, named Margaret, who married Malcolm III in 1069 A.D. She persuaded him to adopt the feudal system of land division, and Saxon and French as court language, instead of Gaelic. She also removed the Celtic influence in the church, in favour of the Roman influence.

Then of James VI first king of Scotland and England, who passed an Act in 1616, banning the use of Gaelic. The Act of Union of 1707, when Scotland became part of Great Britain, but retained its own legal and ecclesiastical systems. The Scottish parliament of the time signing away its independence, for a promise of religious toleration, free trade, and heavy bribes. How the Highlanders rallied to the Stuart cause in 1715 and 1745, but were finally beaten and degraded after Culloden. Many Scots emigrated. Highlanders were forced out again in the early nineteenth century because of Highland clearances. Landlords drove people out of their homes to provide game hunting for a few.

Talk turned to Wales. Of raids by the Scotti, as the Irish were known. Of a Celtic prince, Cunedda, who left his home near Edinburgh to help fight. He founded a Celtic dynasty in north Wales. The last Welsh attempt to drive the English out, by Owain Glyndwr, in 1410 A.D. He died. Then Henry Tudor, Henry VII, who forgot his Welsh roots, an the earlier promise he had made to help their cause. The red dragon on his banner was the symbol of the seventh century Cadwalader. His son was Henry VIII, who made Wales join England in 1536, and then suppressed the Welsh language.

What is it about the Celts, that they often betray their own cause, Conn?

How, he said, do I answer that one? It must be Celtic adaptability, opportunism, mischief, contrariness? What do you think, Erin?

Probably it has nothing to do with being Celtic. It's a symptom of power hungry people, called deceit.

Of course it is, said Conn, and they clinked glasses.

After lunch they returned to the taxi. Conn said that he would explain why the Celt is basically not materialistic. Even the ones that have fallen for materialism have a gut feeling that they could do without all of it, if they had to. It is because there is no verb TO HAVE in Gaelic. The reason why Celts are more spiritual and mystic is because, in Gaelic, as in other Celtic languages, there is more than one way of expressing the verb TO BE. There is no simplistic way of just being. Being, for the Celt, is a variable.

There were passengers and Celtic talk ceased. They witnessed a difference of opinion between mother and child about the purchase of an expensive plastic toy. Their exit prompted an anecdote from Conn. I remember one Christmas going to visit my nephews and nieces. I did not buy them anything from a shop. Instead, I painted a wooden stick gold. I stuck glass jewels on it. I told them that it was a magic stick and they had to use it very carefully. I spent the rest of the evening in a wonderland of childrens' fantasy while I watched them play with the stick. The gift of magic in a child's world is precious.

My nephews and nieces are not children of my sister and brothers, I was an only child. They are the children of my cousins. I am told that I am their favourite uncle. Another tradition at Christmastime and birthdays is Conn's story. Every year I tell a story, tailor made to fit the child. They even remember the story I told them the previous year, but they don't remember the presents they got. It's funny, they expect these stories, even when they are older. It has shown me how important are the threads of tradition.

You, Conn, an only child?

Yes, and what a privilege it was. Spoiled, they're called, but it isn't spoiling it's overprivileged. They have the undivided attention of their parents. They are often precocious because of the time they spend in adult company. They have none of the scars left by sibling rivalry. When I was invited to dinner by my schoolfriends I could feel the tension as soon as we sat down. Whose turn was first, who was getting the most; who pushed; who, who, who. The struggle for priority amazed and bewildered me. When I had dinner at home, it was peaceful and civilised. I never had to strive for place.

Well, that's the trouble with only children, Conn, they don't know how to share, winked Erin.

Not at all. I found it easy to share, it was a novel experience for me. The poor little buggers who always had to share are the ones who find it difficult. It was funny how at school, my friends would always want me to be their brother in our games; they would quarrel about it. I had the opportunity to select my brothers and sisters at school without the inconvenience of taking them home at night. Another thing, only children are very observant. They have the time and freedom to be so. In a large family there is too much hustle, bustle, and noise to perfect your talent for observation. You don't have to strive for sibling success, you can only be compared with yourself. You don't have built in playmates but you do have personal security. And the one person that you know very well, is yourself.

I can only agree with you Conn, said Erin. I'm an only child too.

The day was ending; promise of more Celtic talk tomorrow. An elderly, obstinately refined, couple hired the taxi. Oh, oh, said Conn, they are going to call me – my good man. They did. Conn winked, Erin smiled. He spoke to her quietly, out of the corner of his mouth. These people use to expect curbside service; they would not go into a shop, in case it meant mixing with the locals. The poor bloody shopkeeper had to come out to take the order, then take it back to the car; nor forgetting to tug his forelock if he wanted their business. Shit, said Erin. Precisely, said Conn. The elderly duo described in loud voices, for Conn's benefit, lands they used to own near Dublin. Yes, you could drive for twenty minutes from the road until you reached the door of the house. Conn turned around and humbled his voice. Ah, I used to have a car like that sir, but I traded it in.

They arrived outside Mrs. O'Hagan's house. Erin had tears on her cheeks from suppressed laughter. I haven't laughed so hard since I heard your friends in the pub the other day talking about Connemara. They said that the two occupations there are fishing and fucking – and in the winter there are no fish!

Ah, that's hardly fair on Connemara; it's a beautiful place. But then I seem to remember that the conversation had turned slightly sexist; running down all things feminine. Time to go in and find out if your landlady has something to say; or has to say something.

She was moody yesterday, said Erin.

Oh, you'll get used to that. Brooding is a national pastime here. How's David?

Old enough to look after himself. We talk in the evenings. Mostly about my daily education. It helps me to digest what I have learned if I use him as a sounding board. It's new information for him too, and he loves to process it. Damn, I forgot, I can't come for my lesson tomorrow. David has to return to England soon, and he wants to go to the races tomorrow.

Well, the next day then, said Conn. Back a winner for me.

Mrs O'Hagan stood on sentry duty in the hallway. She reported that Patrick and David were talking in the front room. She disapproved of Erin riding around all day in Conn's taxi. Such nice young men in there, and you spending all that time with that rascal, Conn.

Erin had ammunition, courtesy of Conn.

Proverbs, chapter 17, verse 2: A merry heart doeth good, like a medicine. Good evening, Mrs. O'Hagan. Erin walked into the front room. Black hair intermingled with sandy blond as David and Patrick leaned towards each other in conversation. They were discussing history as it had affected the Jews.

David, you haven't discussed this with me.

He looked up. You haven't asked.

Carry on, she commented. I need all my concentration for the Celts right now.

The men continued. Erin went to make some tea and left the door open. Desmond wandered in, work weary. She nodded towards the open door. He listened . . . the Jews turned to money lending because usury was forbidden by the Christian church. In the Middle Ages they financed construction and wars in Europe, and they were periodically persecuted by communities who were suspicious of their religion and culture; and who owed them money.

That's a nice mixture, said Desmond, construction and wars. Erin, we have missed you at the pub this week. Especially Kelly. He likes your controversy.

It's the Celts, Dad. I come home in the evening, talk to David during dinner; have a hot bath; and go to bed. I can't take any more conversation – really. But I do miss seeing you. Although we do have our fifteen minutes in the morning. Desmond put his hand over hers and smiled. He didn't have to say anything. Erin could tell that he was pleased to have her around, he made no more demands than that.

. . . Jewishness is a cultural rather than a racial state, David continued. The Jews now in Israel come from a great variety of racial backgrounds. It was the strength of religion, family, and rules of behaviour that kept us together throughout history. Like a Roman Catholic, a Jew cannot surrender his religion. Like the Celts, they were, historically, tribal people. The times when they emerged as a nation were under the leadership of great kings. Saul united us; David nurtured us; and under Solomon we prospered. After he died in 920 B.C.E. – before the Christian era – our nation split into Israel in the north; Judah in the south.

Didn't the Assyrians move in? asked Patrick.

Yes, Sargon II conquered Israel in 721 B.C.E. and ten tribes; the so called lost tribes, were deported.

Some people think that one of them made it to Ireland, commented Patrick. The name *Tara* was said to be a corruption of the word *Torah*. It wasn't exactly a tribe. The prophet, Jeremiah, was shipwrecked here, the story goes, and he instructed Finn McCool in the ways and laws of his people.

In the kitchen Desmond raised an eyebrow. A James Joyce character said that there was no anti-Semitism in Ireland, because there were no Jews to speak of. But there was a Jewish Mayor of Dublin, once – Robert Briscoe . . . Erin put a finger to her lips.

. . . the next upheaval came in 595 B.C.E. when Nebuchadnezzar II captured Jerusalem and sent many Jewish prisoners to Babylon. When a revolt flared up in 586 B.C.E he destroyed Jerusalem, and sent even more Jews into exile. Ten thousand families.

They went to New York, said Desmond. Sh! said Erin.

Erin told me some of the history you taught her, said David. I hadn't realised that so many native Irish had gone into exile.

Persecution, famine, death as well. The numbers can't compare with the Holocaust, but the suffering is mutual.

As was the move to America, said Patrick.

Yes, said David. American-Irish and American-Jews were able to pressure England for independent statehood. 1948 was a key year.

Not for the Palestinian Arabs, muttered Desmond.

Nor the Northern Irish Catholics, said Erin. She took in the tea.

The agreement was that Irish and Jewish people thrived in the U.S.A. when and where they were able to flourish. Patrick's dad could remember the No Irish signs that went up when jobs were scarce. David's dad still talked of the insidious qualities of anti-Semitism; even though he was a successful medical specialist. Patrick kidded David that the Romans conquered and ruled Palestine instead of Ireland. It was a question of position, and you were nearer.

Well, said David, you got the English – because you were nearer.

David's family was from Poland. When Russia annexed Poland, the Ukraine and Lithuania, at the end of the eighteenth century; they made a Pale settlement in the rural areas that the Jews had to remain in. Nicholas II in 1855 allowed Jews to leave the Pale if they wished to. They could settle or study elsewhere. David's great-grandfather not only left the settlement, but decided to go to England, in case the Russians rescinded. He was right. After Alexander II was assassinated in 1881, pogroms continued and spread. We were spared the horrors of Nazi Europe, he sighed.

On a lighter note, said Erin, raising her cup, the Yiddish proverb says: If God lived on earth, people would break his windows. Another proverb, origin unknown says; It is optimistic of the devil to think that he can make people worse than already are. David, tell Patrick about the prayer that Jewish men say where they give thanks to God that they were not born a woman.

He doesn't have to, said Patrick. I had a Jewish girlfriend and she told me all about it. Maybe then, we could discuss the merits of Irish and Jewish mothers; they certainly have contributed a great deal to family cohesiveness for generations. The silent strength.

Not so silent, said David. Patrick laughed.

Irish men, Erin continued, have a reverence for their mothers that doesn't always extend to their wives. But then the wives become mothers and get the same reverence from their sons. Jewish mothers secretly believe that no woman born is good enough for their son. What harbours this basic distrust of all women, why is it that Irish and Jewish men have a reputation for an inability to commit themselves to a woman? She winked, present company excepted, of course.

David turned to Patrick. Shall we put cyanide in her tea now, or later?

Why wait? he answered. Desmond wandered in and wondered why they were all laughing.

The following morning Erin woke early and drifted in and out of sleep. She hit that paralytic state where you hear a voice or a movement in the room and try to see who is there. She couldn't lift her head, because her neck muscles were cemented to the pillow. Her eyelids were welded shut. She felt completely helpless. Consciousness connected and she opened her eyes and looked at the clock. The first twenty minutes of her day had not gone smoothly. This was an omen.

The Irish love and understand horses. The Celts worshipped the horse goddess Epona, and the Annual Dublin Horse Show is a celebration in her honour. Bloodstock sales, competition, and showmanship. A five day orgy of horseflesh. David had hired Conn's taxi to take them to the Show while Erin protested that she thought she was just going to the races. There will be some races, placated David. I'll see you tomorrow, Erin, and we'll drown in Celtic mythology, promised Conn, and he was gone.

Erin was aware of the horsey sat among the cosmopolitan hustle and bustle of the show. There were some good looking animals around, man and beast. A group of tweedy young men recognised David with loud voices. They were university acquaintances and she could detect a patronising tone. What, David, are you doing here; and who is this? She noticed that he melded his words with theirs in a unity of group. She felt restless.

They were over from England specifically for the show. She kicked the dirt. It looks like the Twit of the Year competition, she thought.

A stalking cap approached her. What brings you here?

It's not a what, it's a who. David.

Are you interested in riding? Horses? Racing?

Oh, yes, I like racing. All that sweaty horseflesh rushing by, and the man riding astride, and bouncing up and down. The thrust of the animals moving forward, very stimulating.

He wiped a trace of sweat from his upper lip. Do you ride?

No, but I like to watch. The women in their starchy outfits bouncing rhythmically up and down on their horses. Quite a stimulation to the lower lip, without the emotional involvement. He laughed and changed his body posture.

Erin wondered how she would extricate herself before the rockets began firing from his groin. A quick glance from the corner of her eye brought Michael O'Neill into focus. But it was Kevin who bounded over and freed her. He gave her a big hug and greeting and bundled her away. You looked like you needed rescuing from Major Tweedy there.

I did, thank you Kevin, chivalry on a white steed.

Michael was standing next to a pert, blond girl. We need you, said Kevin. That's my girlfriend and Michael doesn't like her. Anyway we haven't seen you for a while with all this education.

Michael took Erin by the arm and steered her away from the blond girl. You may find this hard to believe, but I am pleased to see you Miss O'Brien.

Erin turned to Kevin. Are you going to introduce me?

Shannon positioned herself next to Michael, who said, between gritted teeth; Get her away, she's driving me nuts.

Shannon played with her earring, oblivious to his slurs. My earring won't stay. The hole must have closed up because there wasn't anything in there.

Too bad that didn't happen to the other openings in her body, commented Michael. Erin ginned. So did Shannon, and she wriggled around.

I think Shannon is cold, said Kevin. I'm going to take her inside.

Good, said his brother. She made appreciative noises and clung to Kevin, who didn't know whether to look proud or embarrassed.

Look at how she is dressed for a horse show. High heels, skirt up to her arse, and no coat. What are you smiling at?

Michael O'Neill do you not know that women are biologically programmed to attract men, so that the species will survive? What you see is her attempt to be feminine and alluring, so that men will be attracted to her.

She irritates me. I find her silly and immature. Kevin falls for it, maybe he wants to, but I am not fooled. I would hate to have to rely on that one in an emergency. All that giggling and fluttering and fooling around; she would be more of a hindrance than a help.

Michael, you can't judge women by the way you think they would measure up in an emergency.

What about your biological program, Erin, I don't see you carrying on like that.

No, I don't wiggle and I don't flutter my eyelashes. I suppose I cut all the frills and go for the direct approach. I look him straight in the eye and say – let's hit the sack! Michael smiled through cobalt eyes. However, said Erin, the average girl would rather have beauty than brains; because the average man can see, better than he can think.

Do you know, said Michael, changing the subject, there was a dispute once between the Irish Show Jumping Association and its Equestrian Federation? It was about the appointment of the chef d'equipe for the Nations' Cup team. The dispute went back to 1976, when it was agreed – reluctantly it seems – that any Irish team containing two or more army riders would have an army chef d'equipe. The team had two civilian and two army riders; a civilian was chosen; there was bad feeling. It'll flame up again.

It wouldn't be an Irish show if there wasn't some disagreement, said Erin. Do you like the name of the show jumping arena – Ballsbridge – and one of the judges was called Dungworth.

Love it, said Erin, but I missed the jumping.

You didn't miss anything, we came in second, said Michael. However, if we hurry we will catch the Inter-Hunt steeplechase.

The rain drizzled down while they squelched over well trodden ground, and sought intimate shelter under an umbrella. Now what would I do with you if you were in high heels and a chiffon dress? asked Michael. The steeplechase, which had originated in Ireland, was wild. It was knock-out relay competition, between teams from different Irish hunts. The pace was furious. The fence jumps in the slippery arena were tricky. The rivalry, hot.

At the speed they're going it looks like they are running between pubs, not churches, said Erin. She stayed, toe deep in wet oozy mud, with Michael's grip around her arms tightening as each hurdle was cleared. Shannon and Kevin found them. She was now wearing a blanket around her shoulders and boots on her feet. Kevin tried to make it a foursome huddle, but Michael steered Erin away.

Why, I do believe we are interrupting, said Kevin.

You are, said Michael.

When the racing was finished and rain had stopped, he put away the umbrella, and they sat on a bench. He asked her why she had never ridden. She told him that she would want a promise from the horse that it wouldn't throw her. He commented that if dogs could talk they would not be half so popular. He said that he would take her riding when David had gone. Speak of the devil, he appeared from behind a tent with one of his tweedy friends. Introductions were made, Michael nodded. David had been invited for dinner and the tweedy man wanted Erin to join them. Michael made excuses for her and said that they were just leaving. Erin gave a limp, goodbye wave. Under any other circumstances, I would have spoken up, she said.

You would not have been safe with the tweedy twit, he looked like the shoe fetish type to me. I think that he would have been more than turned on by your mud soaked brogues, he squeezed her. Do we have a date to go riding?

No, we have an appointment, she answered.

Erin sat in the front seat of Conn's taxi and pushed her elbows together behind her back. I didn't get a chance to back a horse for you, Conn. I spent most of the time walking around, following people, and listening to horse talk.

Never mind, we can play a few races at the red lights with the pedestrians. I hear that you and Michael were cozying up.

Pub gossip, scoffed Erin.

Now there's two different characters from the same mould. Carefree Kevin and quiet Michael. There's a touch of the ruthless about him. But they both have hearts of gold. Then there's Rory, the eldest. He's a gem, but spoken for. A priest. A sad loss for the female population. Still, I have my hopes. I did observe a priest the other day, having a quietly personal chat with a Japanese tourist. Around the topic of any extra rubber barriers he might have. A smile of realisation spread across Erin's face as she appreciated that a Japanese tourist was least likely to be a fellow Catholic. There is a no fury like a vested interest masquerading as a moral principle.

Conn packed as many passengers into one morning as he could. He was aided by the authorities who had decided to change the bus timetable. The new times were spaced at maximum inconvenience to the travelling public. Conn merely picked up the masses who had missed the buses. Do you know these changes were ordered by the bureaucracy, just to remind us that they are all still there? I was in a toilet in a government building the other day. A message on the wall said; Right now you are the only man in the government who knows what he is doing.

The afternoon was devoted to Celtic mythology. The two pitfalls are; that these stories were recorded generations after they were first told; and monks recorded them. Without doubt, they enjoyed their task; but they must have experienced some guilt in re-telling pagan stories. We do not know how, or if, they changed them. The monks first began writing in the sixth and seventh centuries A.D., but the plundering Vikings destroyed many records. The twelfth century saw another effort at preserving the mythology. There was Táin Bó Cúlaigne the work of Maelmuiri at Clonmacnoise, in 1106. It fell into three groups. Tuatha De Dannan stories about fairies and wizards. The Ulster Cycle, with King Conchobar, the Red Branch knights, and Cu Culainn. Upper class heroism. Thirdly, the Fenian Cycle, Finn MacCumhaill (McCool),

Ossian, and the Fianna warriors. More romantic and the favourite of the ordinary people. Leabhar Gabhala – The Book of Leinster – was written in the middle of the twelfth century by the Bishop of Kildare, Finn McGorman, and Aed MacCriffan, at Terryglass, in County Galway. They tried to tie in the history of Ireland with biblical history.

Of course, all this mythology loses some of its beauty in translation. It will help you to know that there are some common themes. Clairvoyance and prediction are used a lot. Particularly about a hero, his birth, and future. His coming usually brings death or misfortune to some relative. His mother is often kept prisoner, forced to leave home, or appears to be barren. A hero's conception is not usually a normal process. His natural father may be a stranger or foreigner. Sometimes he is disguised. One conception is even linked to something the mother swallowed. They can also be incestuous. The birth is often unusual. It can be synchronised with a natural occurrence. The hero's life may be threatened at birth and his parents may change. Animals may play a significant part in his birth of life. Finding a name may present a problem. Is that enough for you, Erin?

Well, it wouldn't do for these heroes to be ordinary, she said.

You will have to do some of your own reading, I can only tell you a few. The book of Leinster has a story about an Ulster farmer who boasted, that his wife, Macha, could outrun king Conchobar's horses. She did, even though pregnant. At then end of the race, exhausted, she gave birth to twins and died. The name of Ulster's royal residence was Emain Macha; Twins of Macha.

Why didn't she tell her husband and the king, to go to hell? asked Erin.

A question of honour, said Conn, but she did curse all Ulstermen to the ninth generation, before she died. She said that in their time of greatest difficulty, they would be as a weak as a woman in childbirth; for nine days. The hero Cu Culainn was not born in Ulster, he was there by fosterage; so was not subject to the curse. Arguments were frequent. King Conchobar of Ulster had frequent fallings out with King Ailill and Queen Maeve of Connacht. Cattle or bulls were often the cause of a disagreement. A famous story is the Cattle Raid of Cooley; I won't go into details.

At sometime this Queen Maeve tried to persuade Ferdia to fight Cu Culainn. She offered her daughter Finnabhair, in marriage. She also offered him – my own friendly thighs on top of that – if needs be. She was eventually killed by a nephew; who, angry at a remark she had made, fired a hard ball of cheese at her forehead, from a sling.

What a way to go, said Erin.

Cu Culainn went violently. Being a hero, he wanted to die standing up. In his death throes, he bound himself to a stone pillar. He was the victim of a geis, or taboo. He found himself in a situation where his taboos were unavoidable, so was killed by a combination of trickery and treachery. Remember my introduction? Well, here's a brief run down on this hero. It was said that his birth was the result of an incestuous union between Conchobar and his daughter. Twin foals, born at the same time, became his horses later. As a young boy he goes to Emain Macha as a foster child. There, he fights many youths who tease him, defeating them all. He kills a savage hound that attacks him and then offers to perform the same services as the dog. His name is changed from Setanta to Cu Culainn – Culainn's hound. A druid called Cathbadh prophesies his life will be short, but his fame, long. In battle, a change comes over him. His head revolves on his neck; his hair stands stiffly with sparks of fire; one eye becomes very small, the other, very large; his mouth widens to his ears.

I would think that his opponents would die of fright, said Erin.

He goes to Scotland, to train with the Amazonian, Aife. She becomes pregnant with Ferdia, later killed by his father. Towards the end he said; I care not if my life has only the span of a day and a night, if my deeds be spoken of by the men of Ireland. When he dies, he is beheaded; an old Celtic custom. His body buried at Emain Macha, his head at Tara. He is the typical Celtic warrior hero. Brave, courageous, honourable, physically handsome, arrogant, respectful to women.

Conchobhar was a king, not necessarily a hero. As king, he was treated as a terrestrial god. His rights included the use of a man's wife during a visit, plus the privilege of sleeping with any Ulster bride on her wedding night.

One assumes, commented Erin, that he did not exercise these rights completely.

It could have been very time consuming, and tiring, said Conn. After the kings had gone, the tradition continued. Irish landlords were known to have pursued the same rights with tenants' wives. The Fianna had the same prerogative over tribal women.

The stories of the Fianna and Finn McCool were more romantic than heroic. They were transient henchmen, guarding, and granting justice, and generally helping out. They were also hunters, and the countryside was their home; but for the six winter months they had to rely on the kindness of the local population. They had a slogan; Truth in our hearts, strength in our arms and fulfilment in our tongues.

The story of Diarmaid (Dermot) and Grainne (Grania), is from the Fianna. She was promised to Finn but fell in love with a younger man, and she persuaded him to elope with her. They had to keep moving to avoid the angry Finn, through Connacht and Munster. Dolmens in the area are known as beds of Diarmaid and Grainne. He would not sleep with her for quite some time, as a mark of respect for Finn.

But he didn't know, so what good did that do? asked Erin.

You have to think like these ancient people, he replied. Anyway, eventually Finn was persuaded to stop his pursuit and the couple settled down. Grainne had four sons and a daughter, but they were not destined for happy ever after. Years later, Diarmaid is badly wounded by a boar, and Finn, hunting nearby, twice allows healing water to trickle through his fingers. Diarmaid dies form his wounds and Finn has his revenge.

Old sod, said Erin. There's a lot of Guinevere and Lancelot in this story too, have you got any more?

Hundreds, he replied, but I will have to pick and choose.

Medhbh or Maeve was a queen and a goddess. A lusty, turbulent, female, reminiscent of strong, aggressive, Celtic women. She represented war and fertility. Kings at Tara were supposed to mate with her as part of the ritual of kingship. She appeared as a hag, but when bedded with the king became a beautiful woman. This was symbolic of the barren land that blooms. She cohabited ritually with nine kings, and it was said of her – never was she without one man in the shadow of another. By uniting with Maeve, a king became one with his land. Her usual lover was Fergus, quite a man. He ate seven times as much as a normal man. He was seven hundred times as strong. His nose, mouth, and penis, measured seven fingers; and his scrotum was the size of a sack of flour.

How tall was he? asked Erin, and they both laughed.

It was said that when Maeve was not available, he needed seven women to satisfy him.

All at once? she queried.

Four hundred Celtic gods have been identified. There was no supreme god and many of them had duplicate functions and forms. Badhbh, another war goddess, incorporated Nemhain, Morrighan, and Mach. They frequently appeared as crows, an omen of death, as they are in North American Indian mythology. Another goddess who was in triplicate (she had three heads) was Ellen. She was associated with death and ordered sacrifices to keep her in her underground home.

Lugh, or Lug was the god of war, manual arts, and commerce. His name meant shining one. The festival dedicated to him, Lughnasadh, was held on hilltops on August 1. You can find remnants of his name in the towns of Lyons and Laon, in France, Leiden in Holland, Leignitz, in Silesia.

Dagdha was an all purpose god. Druidism, music and knowledge were his domains. His wife, or mistress, Boann, named her three sons; crying music, sleeping music, and laughing music. She was wed to another, so to hide her union with Dagdha, they caused the sun to stand still. Their son, Oenghus, was conceived and born on the same day. Dagdha had three daughters all called Brighid. One was goddess of poetry, one of healing, one of smithing. Oghma, his son, was a god of learning. The Ogham alphabet was named after him.

Another god associated with healing was Diancecht. His

chanting over well waters gave them healing powers. Legend says that he killed his son, Midach, because he was jealous of his medical ability. Three hundred and sixty five herbs grew on his grave, each associated with healing. His sister, Airmedha, classified them according to their use. This made the father jealous and he destroyed her work.

Cernunnos, the horned one, was an ancient god. He was shown with antlers or the horns of a ram or bull. He sat cross legged and wore a torque. He was accompanied by a ram-headed serpent, a bull and a stag. He was associated with fertility and possessions. He was probably the model that early Christians used for Satan. Manannan, son of Lir, was a sea god and gave his name to the Isle of Man. Belenus was associated with the sun, fire and hot springs. He is probably connected to the Phoenician sun god, Baal. Belenius' festival was Beltene and was celebrated on May 1. I've had enough of this god talk, let's take a break.

It was a fine day and the pub had a small garden at the back, with a couple of chairs and a casually placed table. Conn slaked his thirst, Erin sipped a cider. She continued, after some casual conversation, I have heard of these pagan festivals, but I don't know where, or how.

I am not sure of the how myself, but I can tell you the where and when, he replied. they were seasonal celebrations. Imbolc was celebrated on February 1, at Tlachta, in County Meath. It was a festival of birth and renewal. The goddess involved, was Brighid, patroness of flocks and fertility. Beltaine was celebrated on May 1, it was a festival of fire and purification. The god Belenos was the patron. Ceremonies included driving cattle between two fires to purify them. The great assembly at Uisnech was held at this time. August 1, was a summer festival, Lughnasadh, patronised by the god, Lug. It was celebrated on hilltops at Carmun and Tailtiu. I can remember the time, he continued, when young people would dance on the slabs of megalithic tombs, with garlands in their hair, to celebrate midsummer's eve. Then cam Samhain, on November 1, celebrated the evening before. It marked the beginning of winter. Spirits of the dead roamed around and had to be placated with sacrifices. At Tara, the feis, a parliament, was held every three years at Samhain. Important decisions were made there. By the way, all these festivals were times of truce, in any dispute. The festivals have lingered too, but their original intent is dormant.

The Celtic year was divided by these four festivals. In Scotland, quarter days still fall in November, February, May, and August. Calendar changes have meant that they are no longer the first of the month, but they are times of reckoning and payment. Celtic time was marked by nights, not days. Fifteen nights were called the light half of the moon; and fifteen nights, the dark half of the moon. The bright half was a beneficial time, and the dark half had to be treated cautiously. There were sixty two lunar months, and two inter-calary months, inserted alternatively, at intervals of two and a half, and three years. The Celts also used the vigessimal system of counting by twenties. It survived as one score, meaning twenty. In the past, age was always referred to in terms of score. An eighty year old was four score years. The French for eighty is quatre-vingt, or four twenties. And I remember, said Erin, when there were twenty shillings to the pound.

Conn waved a pause, while he finished his glass of beer. We can sit here a bit, until the blood alcohol level subsides.

Tell me about the fairies, the little people, Erin suggested.

Things have been seen and things have been found, replied Conn. A tiny shoe on the Beara Peninsula, by a man on his way to the doctor. A tiny black shoe, two and a half inches long, in the style of the eighteenth century. He gave it to his doctor, and he passed it one to Dr. Edith Somerville, who took it to America when she went on a lecture tour. It was examined at Harvard, and found to have minute hand-made stitches and eyelets. It was made of mouse-skin.

Have they found any matching hats and coats? asked Erin.

Don't mock, now, the little people can hear you. They say fairy folks are in old oaks, he said, looking up at the trees. Remember, magic is fantasy, there is no fantasy in facts. Some say that the little people are the souls of the dead, some say that they are the gods of nature, and some say that they are the Tuatha De Danann, who were driven underground by invaders. If a fairy tries to mislead you, turn your coat inside out. You might see a fairy on the four festival days I just told you about. As for a good time of day; early dawn, sundown, and midnight. They have been known to live among humans but if you strike or scold them three times they return home. Humans who have been to fairyland find that time is deceptive. A few hours there may be many years later.

Almost as if you had gone into outer space and returned, commented Erin.

You can see a fairy through a naturally bored hole in stone. He took one from his pocket. Erin held out her hand. Now, if you don't see one it could be because you haven't had the magic ointment rubbed on your eyelids. You have all the bases covered, she said as she held it up to her eye. She saw several normal sized men trying to squeeze through the back door of the pub; all at the same time. No, it's not fairies, nor leprechauns, but some of my acquaintances who have sniffed me out.

Advance back there, somebody yelled. I've told you twice, I won't be telling you a second time. Conn, how has the world been using you? It has been using me; and nothing in it for me at all, but experience. And what good is experience? It doesn't pay the rent. You know just before Delaney died, he sat bolt upright in bed, looked at everyone and said; was that it? What about the man who lived outside the city in a cave, as a hermit. They said he was an educated man and should have known better. It's the poor sods who have to scrape a living together in the city, who should know better. They don't have the luxury of living alone in a cave. Did he have any furniture? O'Malley's house looks like it was furnished by an explosion at Woolworths. Where is O'Malley? He's duelling with destiny at the betting shop. You know when you point out mistakes to him, he isn't at all resentful, he just repeats them . . . it is better to have a steady income than to be fascinating. Something to do, something to love, and something to hope for; that is what life is all about. A roof over your head, and something in your belly . . . You can't fool all of the people all of the time; but do it just once, and it lasts for as long as the government is in power . . . Power corrupts, but absolute power is more fun . . . All this beer drinking will, hic – be the urination of me . . . Your trouble is that you would rather be ruined by praised than saved by criticism . . .

And your trouble is that you are kind of person who, when it comes to giving, stops at nothing . . .

I think that the alcohol is narrowing the mind and lengthening the tongue, said Conn. When he puts a pound in the collection plate, it isn't a donation, it's an investment . . . Critics paint a sunset with black paint . . . The only reason you are living is to satisfy your curiosity . . . Envy eats nothing but its own heart . . . Flattery is polite contempt . . . Hate is persistent and continuous, and produces nothing . . .

It's goading time; time to go, Erin.

Just when I am enjoying it, she replied. There is an old Irish proverb, she said to one of the arguers, that says; do not attempt to remove an insect from your friend's forehead with an axe. They returned to the taxi.

As they sat with the windows down, Erin cupped her ear. They are singing.

Yes, it's a Dominic Behan song . . . Come all you young fellows – Stay here while I sing – For the love of one's country's a terrible thing – It banishes feeling at the spurt of a flame – And it makes you a part of the patriot game . . . No, I can tell it isn't an old Celtic song, they didn't know about nationalism, she said. Yes, scattered rural communities, and tribal, bless 'em, said Conn, continuing his course. The tribal, social rules were strictly kept. A tribal king who may have ruled over one of the provinces, or more than one tribe, came from a royal family descended from one great-grandfather. But in four generations of polygamous marriage, you could produce a lot of family members. Kings were elected, not inherited, and someone who was not fit for the role, was ritually slain. It may seem cruel, but in some ways it prevented all the surrounding corruption that comes with a weak leader. I'm sure your British history course had lots of examples of that.

But there was a weakness. The elevation to heroic status of the vanquished and the dead. But surely, Erin said, that was a Christian characteristic. You are a very good pupil, he said, and changed the subject.

At Cashel, there is a large cross that stands on a block of granite. Legend says it was a druid altar. It was also used as a coronation stone for Munster kings from 300-1000 A.D. At Tara was the stone called Lia Fail, brought here by the Tuatha De Danann. It made a loud noise when the rightful king stood on it. There were strange rituals associated with the taking over of kingship. Interesting ones? asked Erin.

One story says that a king-elect mated ritually with a white mare. Then the horse and was killed, sliced up, and boiled. The king-elect had to bathe in the broth and drink a cup of it. This ritual is reminiscent of a Hindu ceremony where a king's wife ritually mates with a stallion, or a bull. It was all a symbolic union with nature to ensure good harvests. Ancient Irish kings were supposed to practise three things; truth, mercy, and silence.

Wait a minute, said Erin. How can you say that bathing in the broth of a dead horse, and drinking a cup of it, is reminiscent of a woman mating ritually with a stallion or a bull?

I was, of course, speaking symbolically of the two unions, explained Conn. I think that I have mentioned before that the Celtic caste system is very similar to the Brahman caste system in India.

The Celtic leaders, druids and poets, were also the historians and keepers of the royal genealogy. The poets, or filidh, were also judges and experts on laws and duties. A master poet, or ollam, was legally, the equal of a king. The aes dana, were another privileged group. They included poets physicians, historians, and skilled craftsmen. They were allowed freedom of the road; but nobody else below the rank of noble, could travel outside his tuath without special permission. While the bards wrote poetry and recited tribal history, the filidh composed satire, which was an important weapon against enemies. The bitterest satire was called satire from the hilltop and was actually an elaborate curse.

We still have bards in the pubs and by the fireside, reciting history, said Erin. The Irish oral tradition is still there. It means that they do not easily forget. The filidh still throw around their satire, wit or curse. The deep feeling of shame still exists, if a satisfactory reply fails to leap from the lips. And, there is always this necessity to have the last word.

You are a good pupil, said Conn.

I mentioned physicians, he continued. Some had surprising skills. A seventh century chief sustained what was probably a skull fracture, in battle. A doctor, called Abbot Briccine, used a technique on him called trepanning. Part of Cenn's brain was cut away, an area called the brain of forgetting. When he recovered he had no trouble with learning, and absorbed all the law, history, and poetry that he heard. Physicians were also skilled at stitching wounds, performing caesarian sections, and working in a clean environment. They also used natural healing and herbs in their treatments.

Conn had talked too much; he was becoming restless. I have neglected the superb craftsmen, but time is galloping. The curvilinear designs that were used on jewellery and weapons were dazzling in their intricacy. The final session drew to a close as day lengthened into evening. Between times, Conn had dissected daily current events, wagered on passing pedestrians, and inspired Erin with a wisdom that surpassed understanding. A divergent education, that could only come from individual attention, and free expression.

They pulled up outside Mrs. O'Hagan's house. I have saved the best till last, the Celtic law, the Brehon. The lawgiver, or judge, administered a law that was based on common practice, belief, and tradition. It lasted until the sixteenth century, when Henry VIII abolished it in favour of English law. It was a treacherous and divisive move, and it fractured Irish heritage.

Basically, Brehon judgements were tribal and made men responsible to each other, rather than to the state. A wrong doing was not a civil offence, but a violation of private rights. The offender was ordered to pay a debt to the injured family, not to society as a whole. A criminal's immediate family could be held responsible for his crime. If he did not accept his punishment, his family was disgraced. Fines were levied, according to a man's economic status. If a guarantor was found, he had to be of equal or higher status. He paid a fine if a criminal defaulted, but then had a right to seize the criminal's property. If a wronged person had been rebuked, he had the right to sit at the criminal's door from sunrise to sunset, and fast until the debt was paid. In those days, honour and shame counted for something. For those criminals, who still refused to be penitent, the druids could take final action. They would be excluded from all religious ceremonies. I like it, said Erin. The idea of a wrongdoing being a family responsibility, not an offence against the state. It's Celtic and tribal, not Roman and nationalistic. The punishments are interesting too. They could account for the traditional Irish feeling of a debt that is owing, to be paid, and the embarrassment of being publicly shamed.

Conn saw the curtains move. And finally, Miss O'Brien, I would like you to know that Celtic men were confident and secure enough to allow women certain protective rights. Under Brehon law a woman could obtain a divorce, if her husband was sexually inadequate; if he failed to make her pregnant; if he publicly embarrassed her; if he abused her sexually and verbally; or if he was unfaithful. The Celtic wife also had grounds for divorce, if the husband failed to provide adequate food and drink when relatives called; if he became too fat; if he had a disfiguring disease; if he had an illness with a long recovery period; or if he returned from war with disabling wounds. A divorce could be conditional. The wife could leave and return later if things had improved. Alimony was often awarded to the wife and her dowry returned. She could also be given compensation for the services she had rendered while married. Punitive damages could be awarded to her if applicable.

I'm impressed, said Erin. I knew that you would be, said Conn. Be careful what you come out with in front of the landlady. Some of those pagan bits, she won't approve of. She might misunderstand. Conn waved at the moving curtains.

I know, said Erin, she thinks that lapsed Catholics are a privileged group!

Chapter

FOUR

It was a cloudy, cool, green day when Erin arrived at a local stable for a riding lesson arranged by Michael. She was busy with internal scheming, a plot to excuse herself from the appointment. Then she saw Michael dressed to ride. A swift, two second glance, up and down. A scan of the eye that gives assessment information, a quick, biological value judgement. The visual stimulus processed, the brain response, and a fleeting smile told Erin to abandon her excuses.

The horse is ready, said the stable boy.

I'm not, said Erin. I need tranquillisers.

Do you take those things? asked Michael.

Not for me, for the horse, she replied. I want to be sure that it is calm, even docile. Actually I would prefer one of those wooden types that don't move at all.

As the two men helped her mount, the horse moved its back legs in a semi-circular motion. Erin froze every muscle, except the one that worked her tongue. It's off and I'm not even on!

Just a normal reaction to mounting, reassured Michael.

The two men were giving instructions about reins and control, but she couldn't listen. I am not ready for this. I have to get off.

You're fine, said Michael.

I am having a panic attack, I don't want to continue.

If you shout you might make him nervous, said the stable boy. She slid off the animal's back, the two men stepped forward to help. The stable boy suggested that Michael take her for a ride on his horse, to give her the feel of it. She is right to be cautious, he continued, beginners do have accidents from over confidence.

Reluctantly, Michael agreed. He motioned her to mount in front. I don't want you grabbing me from behind, as soon as the horse moves.

This way you get to put your arms around me, she mocked. He stared straight ahead. Pay attention to the rein control, watch how the animal moves, feel the motion.

Oh, it's a power play, she thought to herself. The horse trotted into a steady gallop, but Erin had her eyes closed. Michael questioned her, she opened her eyes. If she could forget that she was on a horse's back, she could enjoy the fact that Michael was breathing down the back of her neck and squeezing her with every controlling motion. He promised, no jumps. She felt it slow down and obey a silent command to stop.

Michael slid off and left her sitting there. How about a solo ride?

Erin got down quickly in case the horse had heard. She went over to a tree and sat down. Michael attended to the horse, strolled over, and sat next to her. You should try by yourself, you know. She glared. That was only to give you the feel of it.

Oh, I got that. I wasn't completely oblivious to your genitals rubbing against my backside, Mr O'Neill!

Don't flatter yourself, Miss, I didn't even notice.

If that was you not noticing, I wouldn't like to have to cope with you when you do notice, she replied. He strode back to the horse and mounted. He said nothing. When Erin mounted in front he remained silent as he stuffed his sweater between them. I preferred it the other way, she teased. He gave an impatient sigh and galloped the horse back to the stable at top speed.

Whoa . . . how was it? asked the stable boy.

I think that I will postpone my lesson, said Erin. Somehow I am not ready for the joys of riding just yet.

They drove in silence to a nearby pub to meet Kevin for lunch. He was keen to hear about the lesson. When Erin explained, it sounded so funny that even a reluctant Michael laughed. Hey, I must use that set-up on my next girlfriend, said Kevin.

Don't waste money riding, said Erin. Just say to her, if I said that you had a nice body, would you hold it against me? The three of them spent the rest of the afternoon in trivial, convivial, conversation.

Mrs. O'Hagan had agreed to lend her front room to Michael so that he could teach Erin about Christianity in Ireland. She wondered why Rory wasn't the teacher.

Unlike Patrick, who treated her as an equal, or Conn who was gossipy and fun. Michael took on his teaching with an authoritarian air. If his face hadn't been such an attractive assembly of features, Erin believed that her attention would have wandered. He took a deep breath. I asked my brother about pre-Christian religion as a kind of introduction to my topic, he explained.

Who, Kevin?

No, Rory, the priest. He has made a study of these religions.

A little out of his context, isn't it? she queried.

Rory has a curiosity that extends beyond his job. He said that in ancient times, female deities were supreme. They were earth mothers, bringers of life, protectors of nature, whatever. Goddesses like Isis, from Egypt, Astarte, from Syria; the Greek Artemis; the Roman, Diana; the Celtic, Matrona, and so on. He said that Judaism, Christianity, and Islam, introduced the dominant male and suppressed the role of the female. He cleared his throat.

Was this a revelation for you, Michael?

Don't interrupt Erin, or I will lose the thread.

Come on, Michael, loosen up, this isn't a public lecture. Talk to me.

If you want talking, Kevin should be here.

Do you feel awkward digging at the roots of feminism? asked Erin.

You are going off the topic, he answered. No, I think that this suppression of the female deities is very interesting.

Do you know that there is no equivalent noun for the word, misogynist. Aren't we allowed to hate men? Everyone knows what a nymphomaniac is, but what do we call excessive sexual desire in men?

Satyriasis, he answered, and I know that there are probably more men with uncontrollable sexual desires than women, but we aren't here to discuss definitions. She sat back and shrugged. O.K. you want definitions, he responded. What is an ego-maniac? She shook her head. Someone who calls out his own name during sexual intercourse.

She smiled. O.K. Michael, back to the topic.

The Roman Catholic church sort of returned to female veneration by the importance given to the Virgin Mary. It also adapted some of the pagan goddesses. So, Brighid became St. Bridget, or St. Bride; Matrona became Mary; Santan, the holy fire, became St. Ann; Sinclair, the holy light, became St. Clare. It was designated policy, by Pope Gregory the Great in 601 A.D., to take over native pagan sites and festivals. I suppose that converting them was a way of convincing the local population that Christianity was the true way. Rather than wiping out pagan ways and alienating people. Conn must have told you about the pagan festivals.

Yes.

So you know that February I was Imbolc, festival of Spring. Christians converted it to Candlemass on February 2, the celebration of the purification of the Virgin. May 1, Beltaine, when purification fires were lit, was changed to Walpurgis night, celebrated on April 31. It is celebrated mostly in Northern Europe and Scandinavia. Witches and evil spirits are said to roam around on that night. They light bonfires to drive them away. It was named after St. Walpurgis, an English nun who went to Germany in the eighth century. August 1, Lughnasa, is now the Christian Lammas day. Samhain, October 31, night of the spirits, and beginning of winter, is now the Christian All Saints Day, November 1.

What about Easter? asked Erin.

I have notes, said Michael. The name comes from Eostre, ancient goddess of spring. The date was ruled on at the Council of Nicaea in 325 A.D. After much discussion, it was decided that the date cannot fall later than April 25. It is one of our more mobile festivals. It has to be the first Sunday after the full moon, following the vernal equinox. If this day happens to be on a Sunday, then Easter day is next Sunday. Another complication is that the moon in question is a hypothetical one from the ecclesiastical calendar, and usually one or two days later than the moon in the sky.

I see, said Erin, as clear as mud.

Michael looked up from his notes. Rory has an interesting theory that the true birth of Christ was around this time, and we are actually celebrating birth and resurrection. The year 1 A.D., given as Christ's birth, was decided around the sixth century, A.D., and was incorrect. He was really born in 6 B.C. So what is December 25? asked Erin.

It was a pagan Roman festival called the Birthday of the Unconquered Sun. Birthday of the god Mithras, who they borrowed from the Persians. Mithraism has features that were adapted by early Christians. Such as Sunday being a holy day. Baptism, with a holy sign made on the forehead. Miraculous birth, death and resurrection, the immortality of the soul, a last judgement. Mithraism also incorporated Zoroastrianism and Eleusian ritual. The constant struggle between good and evil. A sacramental feast of bread and wine, symbolising flesh and blood. A belief in heaven and hell. Gnostic beliefs were mixed in as well. I guess you can say that early Catholicism had a knack of picking up elements in other religions that had worship appeal. Provided, of course, that they did not conflict with fundamental belief. Doctrine itself, within the church, caused some conflict. The Eastern Church of the Byzantine Empire, from about the fifth century onwards differed in outlook from Rome, and in 1054 A.D. the break became permanent. They excommunicated each other and each Church did their own thing. Mithraism was deliberately and successfully stamped out by Christians by the fourth century A.D.

This is very enlightening, Michael, you have done your homework well.

Don't patronise me, Erin.

Sorry, did it sound that way?

O.K. let's have a break, I'm not used to all this indoors sitting down. He stretched with sleek, feline movements, obviously aware of his provocative body. He smiled confidently at a bemused Erin. Shall we go out for a stroll? She nodded. They talked briefly of world religions. Michael commented that whoever said – There are many religions, but only one morality – had summed it up nicely as far as he was concerned.

As they walked Michael spoke of their family of three brothers. You know what they say about three in a family. The first born is the leader, the second born, the rebel, and the third born, the charmer. That's Rory, me and Kevin, alright. Rory was certainly a leader. Good at schoolwork, sports and physically striking. He was a nice person too; I worshipped him. He was a perfect kid and he crowned this perfection by becoming a priest. My mum was elevated to that envious position, mother of a priest. My dad was proud. I was devastated and betrayed. He could have done anything and everything, and the church took him. Or, as he would tell you, he chose God. The only consolation is, that he is an unorthodox person. I can't say priest, or he would lose his job. He is careful with his conversation. When I ask him awkward questions, he says, Michael, we still don't understand the power of music, and how it affects the brain. It can soothe or it can arouse – and he has a twinkle in his eye. He will never make it to the top, because he refuses to lick any boots, or toe any line. I suppose inasmuch as any priest influences and helps the people he meets, Rory is making a positive stand in this world.

Would he and I hit it off? asked Erin.

I intend to do everything in my power to make sure that you two never meet.

Why?

Because nobody else would get a word in.

The sun shone and the moment was opportune to pause, relax, and enjoy the feeling of warmth invading the body. Michael and Erin sat in silent communication. The sun's rays penetrating to the reptilian brain and inducing a languid, sluggard, state.

They returned an hour later, to a dim room, flushed with the sun's rays. You don't look ready, Erin, to resume the lesson.

No, I have a strange feeling. I feel as if I have been here, or somewhere like this before – with you or someone like you. She had lost him. She knew that he did not understand. It's passed. I don't often have these metaphysical moments. Let's go on with the lesson. It was probably the sun.

He looked at her strangely. Maybe he did feel something odd too, but he would not admit it. There was an unspoken sexuality between Michael and Erin, but they frequently resented each other and the conflicts were many. Michael lacked the native good humour and charm of Kevin; the sensitivity of Patrick, and David's friendliness. It wasn't so much the devilish good looks but the brooding quality that attracted Erin. She was certainly among the favoured few. Michael generally did not trust women. Erin had confided to Conn that she did not know whether to pity or envy the girl of Michael's dreams. Conn astutely observed, that when matter meets anti-matter, they destroy each other.

I must interrupt your thought patterns, Erin. I am ready to talk about the early Irish Christians who we call saints; but who mostly don't have any claim officially to that title. By their works and deeds, they illustrate early Christianity in Ireland.

I am ready, Michael, just gaze into my eyes.

He had learned to field these comments without the trace of a blush that used to be there. I will begin with the obvious one, Saint Patrick.

Ah, said Erin. Rome's way of saying we didn't get you physically, but we will get you spiritually.

Yes, he was a Roman. The son of Calpurnius, a decurion. He lived in a villa with slaves on the west coast of England. The actual place is disputed, but it was subject to raids by the Irish. Patrick was captured on such a raid when he was sixteen, and sold to Miliuc, king of Dalriada, in eastern Ulster. He stayed there for six years, and while minding the sheep his Christian beliefs grew. He dreamed that he would escape, and he did. He left Ireland by boat and landed on the north west coast of France. He ended up in Auxerre in the middle of Gaul, where Germanus lived. He stayed there eight years. Then, in 429 A.D., Pope Celestine sent Germanus on a mission to England, and Patrick went too. He stayed with relatives for three years. A vision persuaded him that he should return to Ireland to spread Christianity. He went back in 432 A.D. Once there he embarked on some kind of marathon for founding churches and baptising the population. His methods were unique and unorthodox, and were to cause him trouble, later. He cursed, he bargained, he used magic to fight magic, with a determination and stubbornness that can only be described as Celtic. You should read about his mission in Ireland. It can bog you down with names, but will also bring a smile to your lips. He wrote the Confessio, an autobiography, in 455 A.D.

It is said that St. Patrick reached Croaghpatrick, the mountain, on Shrove Saturday. While there he fasted, as Christ had. He also argued and bargained with an angel who went back and forth to God with Patrick's requests. After much bickering, six requests were granted. Patrick then insisted that on Judgement Day he alone, should judge the people of Ireland. The request was eventually granted. It was Easter Sunday, and Patrick celebrated mass. Croaghpatrick is still a sacred place to Catholics. Thousands go there every year on a pilgrimage. Some insist on walking up the mountain barefoot as a penance, and their feet get badly cut.

I have never understood this idea of self punishment doing anything to improve one's religious belief, she said. How can self-inflicted pain be proof of your humility? No matter, tell more more about St. Patrick.

There was a story about Oengus, a king of Munster, who was baptised by Patrick at Cashel. The spike of Patrick's crozier accidentally pierced Oengus' foot during the ceremony. Afterwards Patrick asked him why he didn't cry out. Oengus replied that he thought it was part of the ceremony! Patrick then promised that none of his descendants would die from a wound. Also that future kings of Munster would be consecrated bishops. Twenty seven king-bishops ruled from Cashel until 897 A.D. Brian Boru was crowned there in 977 A.D. and his descendant, an O'Brien, gave Cashel to the church in 1101 A.D.

Another story shows a darker side of Patrick. It was said that his sister, Lupait, became pregnant. He was furious, and when she fell to her knees, next to his chariot, he told his charioteer to drive over her. He did, three times! At her burial, Patrick had a requiem sung for her. She had pleaded on behalf of the father, Aedan. So he was punished with a promise that all his future progeny would be sickly.

Patrick established his own church in Armagh, but when he

wanted to die there, an angel said no. He was told that he would have to return to his original place of entry into Ireland, Saul, in County Down. However, he cheated the angel, through no fault of his own. The cart carrying his body broke at Downpatrick, and he was buried there. The best thing about the conversion to Christianity was that it was without conflict. For two hundred years it evolved side by side with Celtic paganism, and eventually Christianity triumphed.

St. Patrick sounds like quite a character, not your run-of-the-mill type of saint.

Not a saint at all, according to Rome, said Michael. None of our pre-medieval saints have ever been officially canonised; not enough information they say. Sour grapes, if you ask me. They never did like our Celtic Catholicism, and they won't give it any official sanction. St. Patrick thrives anyway. March 17 is celebrated as St. Patrick's Day in many countries. The first parade in New York was in 1762. In hundreds of cities in the United States and across the world, March 17 also serves to remind people of their Irish roots.

Many places in Ireland and Scotland bear the name Patrick. If you don't hear the name much it's because we spell it Padraig. From what you have read, what do you think of him? asked Erin.

He didn't always do as he was directed, he did what he thought best. Towards the end of his life, a so called friend betrayed him to one of these ecclesiastical committees. Nothing important, some minor indiscretion, committed in his youth. But they condemned him, and he was very disappointed. It didn't change the fact that he was the right man, at the right time, in the right place. Another missionary sent by Rome, previous to Patrick, returned, having failed in his mission. Patrick had the knack of successfully spreading the word in Ireland, nobody can dispute that. I'm sure that he was a proud man, and pride is a sin, but how many Catholics are perfect? Certainly not some of those popes from the middle ages; and don't get me started on some of the shenanigans that the Vatican has witnessed in recent times, either.

I read about it, said Erin. In fact, I have often thought it strange, that the Vatican, calling for piety and charity for the deprived in this world, was sitting on one of the largest fortunes in Christendom. What would your brother say?

Nothing, he would pretend that he did not hear. That is not a criticism, he is one of the most pious and charitable people I know. That goes for a lot of Irish missionary nuns and priests. If you go to the most forlorn places, the starving in Ethiopia, for example, you will hear the Irish accent of a priest or nun working right in the thick of it. Let's raise our glasses to them, Erin, and have a break.

Michael's time with Erin was limited to a weekend. He wanted to communicate his information continuously, and fluently. A conscientious, and somewhat formal teacher, his intention was to cover the ground, not necessarily plant anything in it. Although he was interested in Erin's comments, he was also irritated by the interruption. He continued, during the lunch break, to talk of early Irish saints.

St. Kevin probably gave the Irish priest his legacy of celibacy and moral chastity. It was said that he was a good looking lad who longed for solitude. He was only twelve when he chased off an ardent girl with nettles. As a young man, women still pursued him. He withdrew to a cave to meditate. A persistent woman followed him there and they argued. The story was that she fell to her death from the edge of the cave.

Or was pushed, said Erin. Hardly a Christian act. If he felt cursed by good looks why didn't he disfigure himself, like St. Brighid, or wear a mask? I wonder why physical appearance has such weight beyond its importance, she continued. Why do we give it such attention?

You have already answered that, Erin, said an impatient Michael. You told me it was because we can see better than we can think. He continued with the saints.

Saint Columba was of royal birth, a great grandson of Niall of the nine hostages. Born in 520 A.D. in County Donegal, he became a master poet. As a foster child, he got his name Columcille, because his foster home was near a church. Although he studied under Enda and Finian, he never subdued his arrogant, royal Celtic nature. When he built a church in an oak wood he faced the chancel North, rather than cut down too many oak trees. He argued with Finian about a book he had borrowed and copied. Finian insisted on the return of the book and the copy. Columba said no. Once, a relative of his sought sanctuary in a church, having killed a man at a fair. The dead man was an employee of king Diarmait. He and Columba came into conflict. A battle resulted at Cooldrevne, and although Columba won, many men died. He volunteered to go into self-imposed exile, with twelve monks. As an extra penance he said that he would never sat foot in Ireland again. They landed first in Oronsay, but the coast of Ireland was still visible, so they went on to Iona. A monastery was founded, and Christianity flourished for thirty years on Iona and northern Scotland, before St. Augustine brought it to England. Unfortunately, in 1561 the Reformed Church of Scotland destroyed books and monuments on Iona that had survived for centuries.

It's called religious zeal, said Erin. Cromwell had it too and destroyed hundreds of ecclesiastical buildings and statues.

Michael went on. In 575 A.D. Columba was called back to Ireland for a meeting at Drumceatt, in County Derry. Remembering his penance not to set foot in Ireland again, he wore shoes filled with soil from Iona, so that technically, his feet would not touch the ground. He travelled with Aedan, king of Alba. At the meeting, the Scottish kingdom of Dalriada officially broke ties with Ireland, and became independent. King Aedan became the first Christian king in Britain. The Scottish monarch and Irish king MacAinmire, joined hands while Columba pronounced that there should be peace in perpetuity between the men of Eirinn and Alba. One item on the agenda concerned bards, who were accused of indulging in satirical verse, only. Columba decided that they should not be banished as a punishment, but only reduced in number. He also suggested that instead of roving around, they should found schools and their guild should be retained. Columba was a great mediator. He lived to be seventy five, a ripe old age for those days.

He was indeed a feisty Celt, said Erin. I read about him last night. Michael paused, he knew that she was going to spring something on him. Erin continued, Apparently when Columba landed on Iona he said that a human sacrifice was necessary for his venture to succeed, very pagan. Michael stared. She went on. An old friend of his, Oran, volunteered. He was buried alive. Michael gulped down his beer. Three days later, Columba ordered the body to be exhumed. Oran opened his eyes when the soil was scraped away and said, There is no wonder in death, nor is Hell as it is reported. Columba ordered him to be buried again, at once. He said; Earth, earth, on Oran's eyes, lest he blab further. Michael continued to drink in silence. Erin couldn't decide whether he was embarrassed because she had read this, or because he hadn't.

She tried to revive the atmosphere. I was in a pub the other day and heard somebody talking about hedonism, when a voice behind me said . . . Well it's all the same God, isn't it?

Although he tried very hard to suppress it, and lowered his head, a smile forced its way up the corners of Michael's mouth. Can I go on? he asked.

Has anyone told you about the Book of Kells? Michael continued.

She nodded. I saw it at Trinity College. It was thought to have been started as a tribute to St. Columba on the bi-centenary of his death. In 797 A.D. It was started by monks on Iona, but moved to the monastery at Kells after the Vikings attacked in 802 A.D. It took about sixty years to complete, and shows some Oriental and Coptic influence. Records show that Egyptian monks came to Ireland around that time, and Irish monks spent time in Egypt. The design work is beautiful and intricate, but the human touch can be found in the margins sometimes. For example . . . thin ink, bad vellum, difficult text . . . there is some devil in this ink . . . I have written this book for the love of the Irish, because I am an Irishman . . .

The seventh and eighth centuries were Ireland's Golden Age, we can be proud of the quality of work and learning achieved then. Irish scholars composed hymns in Latin and Irish, and invented the use of rhyme, at this time. Irishmen went to Europe and re-introduced learning and Christianity to an area where these things had been forgotten. I think they peaked a little early, said Erin, mischievously.

Michael's notes on monks were his sole quest, he continued. An Irish monk called Dungal, went to the court of the Emperor

Charlemagne in 810 A.D. and explained to him that solar eclipses were the result of a converging of the orbits of the moon and the earth, in the path of the sun. This knowledge then lay dormant for quite some time. Another Irish monk, called Virgile, told people in eighth century Bavaria that there was land beyond the Western ocean, and so by implication the world was round. He was ordered to go to Rome to explain this sedition to Pope Zachary. He gave a good explanation to the Pope and convinced him that he was not deliberately preaching sedition. The Pope said that although he believed him, it was not a suitable rumour for a monk to spread; and he should cease.

Catholicism was ever thus, commented Erin.

Another monk who was convinced that land lay westwards, continued Michael, was St. Brendan. He was born in County Kerry, on the Atlantic coast in 484 A.D. He had heard the legend of Hy Brasil, the land said to be visible across the Western ocean, once every seven years. He set out in a Currach with seven companions, and they were gone for seven years. They found land but we don't know if it was Nova Scotia, Florida, or Mexico. It was said to be a land of sunshine and flowers. An account of their journey can be found in Latin manuscripts in Paris, at the 'Bibliotheque Imperiale. Some say that Columbus studied it. He called in to Ireland in 1492 to add some Irishmen to his crew. St. Brendan lived at the monastery in Clonfert, Galway, and died there in 577, aged ninety three.

Erin interrupted, What would persuade a group of men to set out across the Atlantic, in a coracle, to go into unknown places?

Faith, said Michael. Pelagius preached that man had moral effort born of his own initiative. That one ultimately had freedom of choice. This idea of man's good deeds coming from himself, and not by God's hand, was too humanistic for the Vatican Council, and they, with St. Augustine, suppressed and condemned Pelagius. In the mid-ninth century, a scholarly monk, Johnnes Scottus Eriugena, wrote – De Divisione Naturae – it was the first great philosophical work in Western Europe. At the same time Sedulius Scottus re-introduced the Greek language to Europe. With this revival, the classical world was rediscovered.

Look up from your notes a while Michael, said Erin. I want to see the colour of your eyes.

Do you want a break? he asked.

No, I want you to have one. This is all interesting conversation, but you are lecturing me. Talk to me.

I can't. I don't know this by heart.

Talk to me about these Irish monks, what do you think of them?

I'm proud of what they did, and I don't think that they get enough credit for the intellectual and Christian revival they were responsible for. Ireland has the richest early medieval literary heritage in the world.

What else?

It seems to me that Rome and the popes wanted to reduce the impact that these Irish monks made. One pope deliberately sent out his own monks to counteract the influence of the popular Irish monks.

Why? Jealousy?

Probably. Yes, the church is a business with a power structure like all businesses, said Erin, and it is not appropriate for someone to undermine or challenge that structure.

I think, said Michael, that these early Irish monks were confident and adventurous because Ireland was independent and culturally advanced. Their brand of Celtic Christianity was a challenge to Roman Christianity, and all its vested interests. He paused. Thank you, Erin, by talking, I have freed my own thoughts and clarified my own ideas. Yes, there is a difference between fact and opinion.

Indeed, she replied, opinions are so much more illuminating than facts. They are the proof that you are thinking.

In order to sort the sequence of early Christianity, Michael did have to consult his notes again. Fifty years after the crucifixion, Paul made Christianity available to the west by introducing Greek form to the religion. In 313 A.D. Emperor Constantine made Christianity the accepted religion by the Edict of Milan, and Christianity became Romanised. But he didn't glorify Rome, his capital was Constantinople, built on the former Byzantium. In the fifth century A.D. when Roman influences declined, the two places where Christianity hung on were Italy and Ireland. The Celts adopted their own brand of Christianity; simple and ascetic. Look at that word! said Michael, in a moment of revelation. Add an l and you have asceltic. – as Celtic, he repeated.

Erin smiled enigmatically. What happened?

The Synod of Whitby, in 663 A.D., he replied. This meeting was called on the instruction of Rome. The official reason was to discuss technical differences in the Celtic church. The date of Easter, and tonsure (monks' haircut). Actually, it was a power play to discontinue Celtic Christianity. Bishop Colman, Abbot of Lindisfarne, spoke for the Irish Church. Wilfred, Abbot of Ripon, spoke for the Roman church. King Oswy of Northumbria was the moderator, and had the deciding vote. He had been brought up in the Celtic way, his wife, in the Roman way. Having heard all the discussions he decided to award the decision in favour of the Church of Rome, on the grounds that St. Peter was buried there, and Christ had given him the keys of heaven.

Hell's teeth, said Erin. King Oswy obviously didn't know that Peter went to Rome to try and convert some of the thirty thousand Jews there. He was martyred for his trouble. Hardly a credit to the Roman church. If he had a choice he wouldn't have been killed and buried there.

Well, that decision effectively ended the Celtic church in Britain, said Michael. Bishop Colman and sympathetic monks went to Ireland and founded a monastery at Innishbofin, rather than conform to Rome. The pure, simple, ascetic quality went out of Catholicism.

What took its place? asked Erin.

A religion that was materialistic, bureaucratic, conformist, and heading towards the corruption of the sixteenth century popes. That's it Erin . . . He looked up from his notes like a puzzled schoolboy. Not sure whether or not he had done the right thing.

Thank you, Michael, it was illuminating.

Don't mock.

I'm not, do you have any conclusions?

I am a Catholic by upbringing. I do not attack or defend the religion, I accept it. But I am proud that I am an Irish Catholic. I am proud of the Celtic, pure, spiritual, heritage. I am proud that the flame of Christianity was kept burning in Ireland when the rest of Europe was in the dark. I think that you can only teach the truth of religious spiritually through the simplicity of asceticism.

Erin reacted to the serious mood. Did I tell you the story of how a bribe of a box of chocolates stood between me and a Catholic education?

Yes, said Michael, I'm sorry.

Don't be. It wouldn't have suited me anyway. She could feel that he was sombre, brooding.

My curiosity hasn't been stifled, Erin, just because I was raised as a Catholic.

Did I say that?

No. Well, then what is bothering you?

I heard you talking to Patrick last time we were in the pub.

And?

You were discussing the investigative committee that the Jewish scholars set up because of the emotion generated by Christ's death. the committee deliberated on evidence gathered, and deduced that Jesus of Nazareth, was the illegitimate son of Mary and a Roman soldier. Then the Jews were surprised at the furor that this revelation caused, so they decided to withdraw it. You must have been listening very carefully, said Erin.

When I was doing my research, continued Michael, I came across an ancient description of Christ, from a translation of a letter written by Publius Lentulus to the Emperor Tiberius. Here are parts of it . . . a man of stature, somewhat tall and comely, with a very reverent countenance, such as his beholders both love and fear. His hair, the colour of chestnut, full ripe, plain to the ears, whence downwards it is more orient, curling and waving about his shoulders. In the midst of his head is a seam or a partition of his hair after the manner of the Nazarities; his forehead plain and very delicate; his face without spot or wrinkle. His nose and mouth so formed that nothing can be reprehended; his beard thickish; in colour like his hair, not very long, but forked. His look, innocent and mature. His eyes, grey, clear, and quick.

That is fascinating, Michael. I can almost see Him. But why does this trouble you?

Because, he answered, this is not Semitic colouring. Chestnut hair, with grey eyes? Black hair, with brown eyes would have been closer.

Don't worry about it, said Erin, just think, King Oswy would have had a valid reason for accepting Roman Catholicism! He smiled, laughed and leaned back to break his tension. He looked at his watch. They had missed pub time, but decided to spend the rest of the evening together, just talking. Fornicating minds.

Chapter
FIVE

Erin had told her dad, before they went to the pub that evening, of her plans to go to the United States with Patrick. She planned to stay for a year, and he had assured her that he could find her some kind of teaching position. She explained that there was nothing romantic, it was a business arrangement. She had phoned the news to David, and he thought it was a good idea.

Well, I don't know about you independent women, said Desmond, it seems that you know what you want, and you go for it. Good luck to you. I would like to have seen America myself. I never had the get up and go to get there.

Why don't you come with me? No, not now, I'm too old. Send me some picture post-cards.

I will write to you.

No, don't bother yourself with that.

Now that we have found each other, we must maintain contact. Desmond looked tired, but was about to get his second wind as pub hour approached. He enjoyed his time in the pub each night. The routine was comforting.

Mrs. O'Hagan inquired each day about David. Each time the answer was the same, but she didn't seem to mind. He had to return to London to resume his studies, and he sent his regards. She put her hand to her mouth with a slight gasp and fingered a well worn card he had sent to her, in her apron pocket, as if it were a string of worry beads. Such a nice lad, always time for a chat. He used to listen to my ailments; gave me more time than my own doctor; who I never go to see. Dr. O'Grady has more sense than to listen to her prattle, said Desmond. She didn't hear. She busied about the room with domestic gestures and found a collection of objects to remove. We didn't get the biblical quote, said Erin. No, she was thinking about her young man. She had a soft spot for him, after he had that cold, and she fussed over him.

Kelly appeared at the window, and gave his, come on let's go wave. Desmond stood up and brushed the curtains with a familiar gesture that signalled he was ready. I'll come later, Dad, said Erin. Bring at least one joke for Kelly. It makes his night.

Erin gripped the sides of the chair, stretched out her legs, and closed her eyes. It was switch-off time, blanking the mind. Twenty minutes later she opened her eyes and stared through the window. A tree caught her attention. Suddenly, a shower of leaves came down in unison. No wind to move them. It was as if they had a natural, spontaneous, effort to discharge themselves. A silent agreement to abort.

When she arrived at the pub, Patrick was discussing Finnegan's Wake with Desmond, who disapproved of the book. Some say it's brilliant gobbledy-gook, others say it's a linguistic delight, but I think the silly old fool suffered a slight stroke and wrote it while his brain cells, in the area of speech, were under pressure.

There they all were – Conn, Desmond, Patrick, Kevin and Kelly. No Michael. Kelly was the first to broach the subject of Erin's departure. In only two short days you'll be gone. We are devastated. We are used to having you around.

Opportunities, said Desmond, seldom come labelled.

What worries me, said Kevin, is that Patrick won't know how to care for her.

I suppose you would, said Kelly.

What does he know, said Erin, he thinks that innuendo is an Italian suppository; Kelly spluttered. And Fellatio is a character in Hamlet, replied Kevin.

I see, Kevin, that you and I go in the same toilets, winked Erin.

She had noticed Michael slip into the pub and stand on the perimeter. Conn went over to talk to him. Have you never wondered why you are here, Michael? Why you were conceived and born, and why the other struggling spermatozoa were unsuccessful? Have you considered what is your purpose on this planet? What is your niche or fulfilment?

Michael looked impatient. No, I have never thought about any of those things. If you are hung up on those questions, Conn, that is your problem.

But Michael, sometimes the key to our understanding, is knowing the right questions to ask. Conn looked over towards Erin. Michael wandered away. Conn commented to Desmond. When we arrive on his earth, we don't come with a set of instructions. In the case of some people, that is a great pity. There is nothing sadder than a misunderstanding.

An old man was rambling on in a repetitious, forgetful, fretful way. Symptomatic of old age, combined with excessive alcohol. People offered to see him home. He protested. He said that he didn't like them. He fastened on to Michael, and clung, leechlike, to his arm. Michael, knew when authority had to usurp sympathy. I am eighty seven, said the old man, barely standing.

You look it, said Michael, steering him towards the door. He moved meekly in the direction of his free ride. Michael did not come back.

He took it badly, said Kevin, but he wouldn't admit it. Michael has always considered people disposable. He says that we are all from the same clay. He would like to punch Patrick out, but he can't find a valid reason. He's taking evening classes now, he doesn't want to work in construction any more. Patrick talks a lot more than he did. Desmond smiles more. Kelly has smartened himself up. I try to be a little more serious. And I hear that Conn is seeing more of a certain widow, lately.

I am, said Conn, but before I get too involved I have to make sure that the first husband died by shooting and wasn't nagged to death!

Erin said – au revoir – to the group. It has been, she added, an education. The glasses clinked.

I would like to propose a toast, said Conn. To Erin, our catalyst. The glasses clinked again, and Desmond explained to a bewildered Kelly.

The morning of the departure was grey and wet. Sheets of rain fell. The heavens are weeping, said Conn. A sleepy Erin, a quiet Desmond, and an energetic looking Patrick arrived at the airport. Goodbyes were brief, emotions sincere. In the taxi, on the way back, Conn was the quiet one. Desmond patted his hand as he left the car. Just remember, Conn, you can take the girl out of Ireland, but you can't take Ireland out of the girl.